Teen Biz Parent Guide

Teen Biz Parent Guide

Teen Biz Parent Guide

Target Evolution, Incorporated
Crystal Victoria, Executive Director
Website: http://targetevolution.org

© Copyright 2024 by Target Evolution, Inc. All rights Reserved.

No part of this book may be reproduced, stored in a retrieval system, or transmitted by any means without the written permission of the author.

Published by Target Evolution, Inc.
Publication Date: April 15, 2024
Print ISBN: 978-1-943240-14-2 (sc)
eBook ISBN: 978-1-943240-15-9
Library of Congress Control Number: 2012904697

Any people depicted in stock imagery provided by Thinkstock are models, and such images are being used for illustrative purposes only.
Certain stock imagery © Thinkstock.

Disclaimer: Because of the dynamic nature of the Internet, any web addresses or links contained in this book may have changed since publication and may no longer be valid. The views expressed in this work are solely those of the author and do not necessarily reflect the views of the publisher, and the publisher hereby disclaims any responsibility for them.

TABLE OF CONTENTS

Section 1: Frequently Asked Questions
Am I an entrepreneurial parent?	11
My kid wants to be an entrepreneur, and I don't know what to do.	12
I want my kid to take over my business or help me manage my business. What do I do?	14
How do I support my kid entrepreneur?	13
Training/Courses	13
Events	13
Pop-Up Shops/Vendor Opportunities	13
Pitching and Pitch Events	14
Networking	14
What's required of me as a parent?	15
Time investment	15
How to help my kid manage a business while they are in school	15
How to manage my kid's business while I work	16
What expenses and costs should I expect?	17
My kid wants to change their product or business. Now what?	22
My kid wants to quit the business or doesn't like being an entrepreneur. Now what?	24
How do I reward my kid without making it too easy?	25
Legal and Tax Implications	26

Section 2: Interviews with Parents of Youth Entrepreneurs
Christy Mannering	43
Iris Pelton	53

Section 3: Template Guide for Teen Biz Workbook
Business Knowledge Assessment	61
Lean Startup	64
Business Plan vs Pitch Deck	65
The Business Model Canvas	69
Teen-Friendly Business Model Canvas	70
Official Business Model Canvas	71
Brand Identity Development	73
Market Research and Validation	78
Startup Budget	82
Financial Projection Calculator	84
Pitch Deck Template	85
One Page Plan and Pitch Notes Worksheet	92

Section 4: Parent Resource Guide
Tips & Tricks for Teaching Money Management	97
Teaching Your Kids Credit	98
Teaching Your Kids Stock Market	99
Books and Online Education	102
Teaching Your Kids Real Estate	103
Additional Resources	105

FOREWORD

To the Parents, The Mentors, and Our Children's First Love,

In an era of rapid technological advancement and ever-evolving career landscapes, the traditional pathways to success are undergoing significant transformation. As we witness the rise of automation and artificial intelligence (AI), it becomes increasingly evident that fostering entrepreneurial skills in our youth is not just beneficial but imperative for their future prosperity.

Welcome to "The Teen Biz Parent Guide"! In this book, we explore the profound impact of entrepreneurship as a career option and also a vital backup plan amidst the shifting tides of technology, "pop culture", and everyday life.

As parents, mentors, and guardians, we have a crucial role in shaping the mindset and skill set of the next generation. In a world where today's jobs may become obsolete tomorrow, equipping our youth with the tools to navigate uncertainty and seize opportunities is paramount. Entrepreneurship emerges as a beacon of resilience, creativity, and adaptability in this ever-changing landscape.

Throughout these pages, we delve into the why and how of cultivating entrepreneurial spirit in our children. We will uncover entrepreneurship's inherent value beyond business, emphasizing its role in fostering critical thinking, problem-solving abilities, and emotional intelligence. From igniting innovative thinking to instilling a sense of self-reliance, the benefits of entrepreneurship extend far beyond financial gains.

Furthermore, we confront the reality of automation and AI, acknowledging both the remarkable advancements they bring and the potential disruptions they pose to traditional career paths. While automation may eliminate certain jobs, it also paves the way for new opportunities and industries yet to be imagined. In this context, entrepreneurship emerges as a resilient and adaptive response to the uncertainties of technological progress.

As we guide our youth toward entrepreneurship, we embrace a holistic approach encompassing education, mentorship, and practical real-world experiences. We empower youth to identify problems as opportunities, embrace failure as a stepping stone to success, and leverage technology as a catalyst for innovation.

Moreover, we recognize the importance of nurturing an entrepreneurial mindset alongside academic pursuits. By fostering curiosity, resilience, and a willingness to take calculated risks, we prepare our children for today's jobs and tomorrow's challenges and opportunities.

In " The Teen Biz Parent Guide", we draw inspiration from real-world examples of young entrepreneurs who have defied the odds, transformed setbacks into stepping stones, and harnessed the power of entrepreneurship to create meaningful impact. Their stories serve as beacons of hope and motivation, illustrating the transformative potential that lies within the heart of every individual, both young and old.

As we embark on this journey together, let us embrace the role of catalysts for change, guiding our youth toward a future brimming with possibilities. Through entrepreneurship, we equip them with the skills, mindset, and resilience needed to navigate the complexities of the modern world and emerge as architects of their destiny.

Join us in unlocking the full potential of tomorrow's entrepreneurs, shaping a future where innovation knows no bounds and every challenge is met with boundless creativity and determination.

START THE "TARGET EVOLUTION" WAY

There are several ways to help your kid start a business and learn how to run and manage it. Some may tell you to start by getting an LLC or filing corporation paperwork for your state; however, entrepreneurship education is very different from how real entrepreneurship and business probably work. At Target Evolution, we believe the best way to teach your kid entrepreneurship is with a product-based business, which helps them build habits and the character conducive to success in any field they choose.

Once they earn over $400 consistently over 3-6 consecutive months or decide they really like being young entrepreneurs, we suggest going through the legal processes according to your local jurisdiction. We highly suggest checking business laws in your city, state, and county and talking to an attorney and accountant because we cannot provide legal advice. To start, position your kids to begin selling a product and then help them develop communication skills, habits, and the character to be entrepreneurs. We have a low-cost Teen Biz Box and online course to help with this step. After this exercise, it'll be easier to decide which direction you should go legally and tax-wise with their business.

Over the last few years, we've seen thousands of kids and teens start a business, change their business, grow a business, and fail at businesses. The most consistent challenge we've observed is kids changing their minds. Change of mind can come with a change of product(s) and, oftentimes, a change of the entire business model. To keep yourself from being exhausted by the multiple changes your kid will go through during this entrepreneurship education process, allow them to be flexible and provide just enough support to see if they like the daily grind of it first. Before investing tens of thousands of dollars and helping them create a whole product line, ensure your kid has the habits, character, and skills to succeed. Next, make sure they like being an entrepreneur and are good at managing emotions and their time.

In this guide, you will hear from parents of kid entrepreneurs and get strategic tips on how to help your kid grow their business while ensuring they have an entrepreneurship education lesson that sticks with them for life and can be transferred to any career or business they choose in the future.

This short, easy-to-read guide includes templates and worksheets from "*The Teen Biz Workbook*", which will help you to work with your family and plan the most crucial steps in helping your kid entrepreneur. *The Teen Biz Parent Guide* is divided into four sections:

1. **FAQ (Frequently Asked Questions)**
2. **Teen Entrepreneur Parent Interviews**
3. **Template Guide for Teen Biz Workbook**
4. **Parent Resources**

Target Evolution is here to help you and your kid navigate the opportunities, changes, and challenges of entrepreneurship along the way! Thank you for choosing us to support your child's entrepreneurial journey!

Let's do this!

With warm regards,

Crystal Victoria, Founder of Target Evolution Incorporated, and

Published Author of 9 books, including "*The Teen Biz Workbook*," "*Teen Biz Parent Guide*," "*Teen Biz Shop: Keys to Success*," and "*Teen Biz Guardians*" Comic Book Series, and a college textbook entitled "*The Entrepreneur's Workbook*."

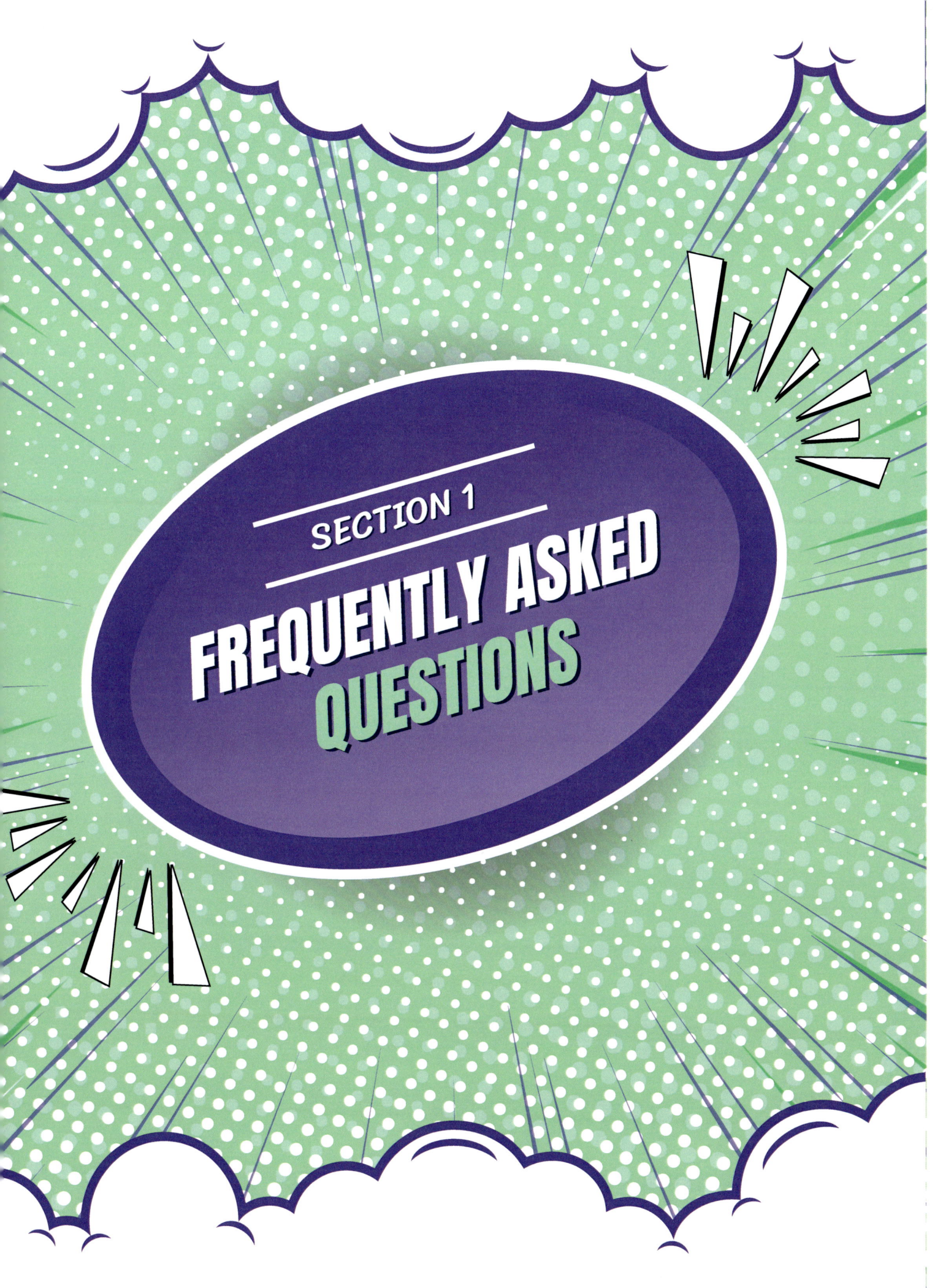

ARE YOU READY TO BE A PARENT OF A KID ENTREPRENEUR?

Supporting a young entrepreneur as a parent requires a specific set of qualities and attitudes. Here are some indicators that you might have the personality traits conducive to helping your kid entrepreneur:

Encouragement and Positivity
You consistently provide encouragement and positive reinforcement, fostering a can-do attitude in your child.

Adaptability
You are open to change and can adapt to new situations, recognizing that entrepreneurship involves a dynamic and evolving journey.

Patience
Supporting a young entrepreneur can be challenging at times. If you are patient and understanding, you can navigate setbacks and challenges with a calm demeanor.

Communication Skills
Effective communication is key. If you can openly discuss ideas, challenges, and goals with your child, it fosters a healthy and supportive environment.

Empathy
You can empathize with your child's experiences, acknowledging their efforts and understanding the emotional aspects of their entrepreneurial journey.

Interest in Learning
You have a genuine interest in learning about your child's business and the world of entrepreneurship, showing curiosity and a willingness to engage in discussions.

Resourcefulness
Being resourceful helps you navigate the various aspects of entrepreneurship, from finding educational materials to connecting with other parents of young entrepreneurs.

Resilience
The ability to bounce back from setbacks is crucial. If you can model resilience for your child, it helps them learn to cope with challenges in their own entrepreneurial endeavors.

Supportive Network
You actively seek and encourage connections with other parents, mentors, or organizations that can provide additional support and resources for your child.

Trust in Your Child's Abilities
You believe in your child's capabilities and trust that they can learn and grow through their entrepreneurial experiences.

Financial Literacy
Understanding basic financial principles can be beneficial when guiding your child in budgeting, managing profits, and making sound financial decisions.

Leadership Skills
You can provide guidance without being overly controlling, allowing your child the autonomy to make decisions and learn from their experiences.

Celebration of Achievements
You celebrate your child's successes, no matter how small, recognizing and reinforcing their achievements in their entrepreneurial journey.

Time Management
Balancing your own commitments with supporting your child's entrepreneurial activities requires effective time management skills.

Teen Biz Parent Guide

Long-Term Perspective

You have a long-term perspective, understanding that entrepreneurship is a developmental process, and success may take time to materialize.

It's important to note that no one is perfect, and parenting is an ongoing learning experience. If you recognize some of these traits in yourself and are willing to develop and strengthen others, you likely have a personality conducive to supporting your kid entrepreneur. Creating an environment that nurtures creativity, resilience, and a passion for learning will contribute significantly to your child's entrepreneurial journey.

My kid wants to be an entrepreneur, and I'm not sure what to do:

It's wonderful that your child has expressed an interest in becoming an entrepreneur. Supporting and nurturing their entrepreneurial spirit can be a rewarding experience. Consider these steps:

Encourage Exploration

Allow your child to explore various interests and activities related to entrepreneurship. This could include attending workshops, joining entrepreneurship clubs at school, or participating in local youth entrepreneurship programs, like the Teen Biz Camp!

Be a Listener

Have open and supportive conversations with your child. Listen to their ideas, aspirations, and any challenges they might be facing. Encourage them to share their thoughts on what they want to achieve as an entrepreneur.

Educate Together

Learn about entrepreneurship alongside your child. This could involve reading books, attending events, or watching educational videos about entrepreneurship. This shared learning experience can strengthen your connection and provide valuable insights.

Facilitate Networking

Help your child connect with other young entrepreneurs or mentors in the entrepreneurial community. Networking can provide inspiration, guidance, and a sense of community for your child.

Teach Financial Literacy

Introduce basic concepts of money management, budgeting, and financial responsibility. Understanding these principles is crucial for any entrepreneur.

Foster Creativity

Encourage creativity and innovation. Provide opportunities for your child to think outside the box, solve problems, and come up with unique ideas. This could involve engaging in creative activities or brainstorming sessions together.

Provide a Safe Space for Failure

Emphasize that failure is a natural part of entrepreneurship. Help your child understand that setbacks are learning opportunities and not reasons to give up. Creating a supportive environment where they feel safe to take risks is crucial.

Set Realistic Expectations

Discuss the realistic expectations and challenges of entrepreneurship. Being transparent about the potential difficulties helps your child develop resilience and a realistic understanding of the entrepreneurial journey.

Celebrate Achievements

Celebrate both small and big achievements. Recognize your child's efforts and accomplishments as they navigate the entrepreneurial path. Positive reinforcement can fuel their motivation.

Provide Practical Experiences

If feasible, involve your child in real-world entrepreneurial experiences. This could include helping with a small business idea, attending local pop-up markets like Acton's Children's Fairs, Lemonade Day, and Teen Biz Pop Up Shops, or participating in entrepreneurial events.

Promote Leadership Skills

Encourage the development of leadership skills, teamwork, and effective communication. These skills are valuable for any entrepreneur.

Be Patient and Supportive

Understand that the entrepreneurial journey can have ups and downs. Be patient, supportive, and available to provide guidance when needed. Your emotional support is invaluable.

Remember, every child is unique, and their entrepreneurial journey may take various forms. The key is to provide a supportive environment, foster a love for learning, and help them develop the skills needed for success. Your involvement and encouragement can make a significant difference in your child's entrepreneurial pursuits.

What exact steps can I take to support my kid entrepreneur?

a. Training/Courses

Target Evolution offers multiple programs and options for training. We offer online and onsite training called Teen Biz Camp, which includes our Teen Biz Box, Teen Biz Workbook, and a quick course to help you and your kid get started. We also have a weekly blog and comic book series, which can help your child learn lessons in a fun engaging way!

b. Events

Check out your local startup and entrepreneurial community in your city. There are coworking spaces with events and opportunities for you to learn and expose your kid to information from people who are entrepreneurs. Chambers of Commerce, Meetup groups, and Eventbrite offer a wide selection of events, as well as local colleges and universities.

c. Pop-Up Shops/Vendor Opportunities

Again, Chambers of Commerce, Meetup groups, and Eventbrite offer an incredible variety of events, as well as local colleges and universities. Consider trade shows, conferences, and small events to be a vendor and do a pop-up shop. Target Evolution also has Pop Up opportunities with our Teen Biz Shop and other events on our website for more information. Also, consider Acton's Children Business Fairs and Lemonade Day.

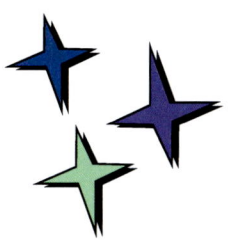

Teen Biz Parent Guide

d. Pitching and Pitch Events

Check out the local startup and entrepreneurial community in your city. There are coworking spaces with events and opportunities for you to learn and expose your kid to information from people who are entrepreneurs.

e. Networking

LinkedIn and Facebook Groups are great social platform options for online professional networking. Also, be sure to check with Chambers of Commerce, Meetup groups, and Eventbrite, as well as local colleges and universities.

I want my kid to take over my business or help me manage my business. They don't seem to be interested. What can I do?

Encouraging your child to take an interest in and eventually manage or take over your business requires a thoughtful and supportive approach. Here are a few strategies:

Understand Their Interests

Begin by understanding your child's interests, passions, and strengths. If your child has different aspirations, try to find a connection between their interests and aspects of the business that align with those passions.

Open Communication

Have an open and honest conversation with your child about your desire for them to be involved in your family business. Ask about their feelings, concerns, and aspirations. This dialogue can provide valuable insights into their perspective.

Educate Them About Your Family Business

Take the time to educate your child about the intricacies of your family business. Provide insights into the industry, the impact of the business on the community, and the potential for growth. A deeper understanding may spark interest.

Hands-On Experience

Offer your child opportunities to gain hands-on experience within your family business. This could involve shadowing you, assisting with specific tasks, or even taking on a small project. Practical exposure may help them better grasp the nature of the business.

Highlight the Family Legacy

If applicable, emphasize the family legacy associated with the business. Discuss the hard work and dedication that went into building the enterprise and the potential for them to contribute to and carry forward that legacy.

Mentorship Opportunities

Introduce your child to mentors or role models within the industry. Sometimes, hearing from other successful individuals in the field can inspire and motivate them to consider a more active role in the business.

Discuss Future Opportunities

Talk about the potential for growth, innovation, and new opportunities within your family business. Highlight how their involvement could contribute to shaping the future of the enterprise.

Emphasize Transferable Skills

Illustrate how the skills they acquire by being involved in your family business can be valuable in various aspects of life, not just within the business context. Entrepreneurial skills are often transferable and applicable in diverse situations.

Professional Development

Encourage your child to pursue relevant education or training that aligns with the business. This can enhance their knowledge and skills, making them more confident about taking on a role in the future.

Set a Succession Plan

If possible, work together to create a succession plan. This plan could outline gradual involvement and responsibilities, providing a clear path for your child to take over or manage your family business over time.

Respect Their Choices

Ultimately, it's essential to respect your child's autonomy and choices. If they are not interested in taking over your family business, consider supporting their chosen path while maintaining open communication about the future.

Seek Professional Advice

Consult with business advisors or professionals who specialize in family businesses. They can provide guidance on navigating family dynamics and succession planning.

Remember that everyone has their unique aspirations, and it's crucial to respect your child's individuality. While it's natural to desire their involvement in the business, creating an environment that fosters genuine interest and passion is key to their long-term commitment and success in the role.

What's required of me as a parent, as it relates to time and costs?

Time Investment

Guidance and Mentorship

Dedicate time to provide guidance and mentorship. Act as a sounding board for their ideas, answer questions, and help them navigate challenges.

Educational Support

Support their learning by helping them understand business concepts, financial literacy, and other skills relevant to entrepreneurship. Consider engaging in joint learning activities. If you don't feel comfortable providing educational support, consider seeking a mentor or advisor from SCORE or a local SBDC (Small Business Development Corporation).

Networking Opportunities

Invest time in creating opportunities for your child to network with other entrepreneurs, mentors, or industry professionals. Networking can open doors and provide valuable insights.

Market Research Assistance

Assist with market research activities. Help them gather information, analyze data, and make informed decisions about their business.

Hands-On Involvement

Be actively involved in aspects of their business where your expertise can contribute. This could include helping with administrative tasks, managing finances, or offering insights into marketing strategies.

Encourage Creativity and Innovation

Spend time fostering creativity and innovation. Engage in brainstorming sessions, encourage them to think outside the box, and help them develop unique ideas.

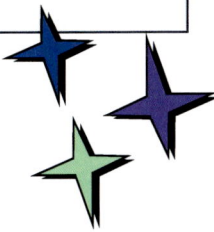

Teen Biz Parent Guide

Participate in Events and Competitions

Attend events, competitions, and other activities related to entrepreneurship with your child. Your presence can provide support and encouragement.

Set Regular Check-Ins

Establish regular check-ins to discuss progress, challenges, and future plans. Consistent communication helps build trust and ensures you are aware of their needs and concerns.

How do I help my kid manage a business while they are in school, and I have to work?

Create a Schedule

Work together to create a schedule that accommodates both school and business responsibilities. Allocate specific time blocks for homework, business tasks, and relaxation. Having a structured schedule can help manage time effectively.

Establish Clear Communication

Maintain open communication with your child. Understand their academic schedule, extracurricular commitments, and the time they can realistically dedicate to the business. Discuss expectations and set realistic goals.

Prioritize Education

Emphasize the importance of education. Ensure that school responsibilities take precedence. Help your child understand the balance between academics and business, ensuring that neither is compromised.

Delegate Responsibilities

Identify specific tasks within the business that can be delegated or outsourced. This could include hiring part-time help or involving other family members. Delegating tasks helps distribute the workload and eases the burden on your child.

Utilize Technology

Leverage technology to streamline business processes. Use online tools and apps for project management, communication, and other business-related tasks. Asana and Monday.com are great tools to begin organizing business processes and tasks.

Encourage Time Management Skills

Teach your child effective time management skills. This includes setting priorities, breaking down tasks into manageable steps, and avoiding procrastination. These skills will be valuable both in school and in managing the business.

Set Realistic Goals

Establish realistic and achievable goals for the business. This ensures that your child can focus on specific tasks without feeling overwhelmed. Celebrate small successes and milestones along the way. Create a vision board to help stay focused on the bigger picture!

Establish Boundaries

Help your child set boundaries to avoid burnout. Ensure they have designated time for rest, relaxation, and social activities. Balancing work and personal life is essential for overall well-being.

Provide Emotional Support

Running a business while in school can be challenging. Offer emotional support, encouragement, and praise for their efforts. Let them know that you are proud of their entrepreneurial spirit and commitment.

Network and Seek Guidance

Connect with other parents whose children are managing businesses while in school. Share experiences and seek advice on how to navigate the unique challenges of balancing education and entrepreneurship.

Flexible Work Arrangements
If your work allows, explore flexible work arrangements that align with your child's schedule. This could involve adjusting your work hours or exploring remote work options to provide additional support.

Teach Financial Literacy
Use the business as an opportunity to teach financial literacy. Help your child understand budgeting, profit margins, and the importance of reinvesting profits wisely. These skills are valuable for both the business and personal finances.

Remember to regularly assess the arrangement, make necessary adjustments, and celebrate achievements. Providing a supportive and collaborative environment can contribute to the success of your child's entrepreneurial endeavors while maintaining focus on their education.

What expenses and costs should I expect?

Educational Resources
Invest in educational resources such as books, courses, or workshops that can enhance their entrepreneurial skills and knowledge.

Business-related Expenses
Allocate budget for business-related expenses, which might include materials, technology, marketing, or other costs associated with their venture.

Networking Events and Memberships
Budget for networking events, memberships, or programs that provide opportunities for your child to connect with other entrepreneurs and professionals.

Professional Advice
Consider consulting with professionals, such as business advisors or mentors, who can provide guidance on the legal, financial, or strategic aspects of their entrepreneurial pursuits.

Travel Expenses
If applicable, budget for travel expenses to attend entrepreneurial events, conferences, or competitions that can broaden their exposure and experience.

Online Presence
Invest in building and maintaining an online presence for their business. This may include costs associated with a website, social media management tools, or other digital marketing expenses.

Financial Planning
Work with your child to develop a financial plan for their business. This includes budgeting, forecasting, and understanding the financial implications of their decisions.

Insurance Coverage
Depending on the nature of the business, consider insurance coverage to protect against potential risks and liabilities.

Legal Support
Budget for legal support if needed, especially when it comes to registering the business, understanding legal obligations, and protecting intellectual property.

Recognition and Rewards
Allocate funds for recognizing and rewarding your child's achievements and milestones. This can provide positive reinforcement and motivation.

Remember to regularly assess the arrangement, make necessary adjustments, and celebrate achievements. Providing a supportive and collaborative environment can contribute to the success of your child's entrepreneurial endeavors while maintaining focus on their education.

Teen Biz Parent Guide

Start with this budget template to help you plan financially. A good rule of thumb is to save and set aside 6-12 months of expenses. Our Teen Biz Camp and Teen Biz Box is a great way to help your child get started simply and inexpensively at a low upfront and monthly cost. However, create a plan that works best for you and your family's situation.

Monthly Budget Template	Cost
Educational Resources	
Business Related Expenses	
Marketing (Website, business cards, flyers, graphic design, digital marketing, social media management tools)	
Technology (Computers, Devices, Software)	
Product Inventory	
Equipment (tools, machines to create the product if applicable)	
Networking and Memberships (Chamber Memberships, Workshops, and Events)	
Professional Advice (Lawyer, Accountant, Consultant, Coach)	
Travel Expenses (Gas, Uber rides, plane tickets)	
Financial Planning (Bookkeeping system	
Insurance (business liability insurance)	
Legal Structure (permits, trademarks, patents, copyrights, articles of incorporation)	
Total	

Is there funding for kid businesses?

Grants and Competitions
Some organizations and foundations offer grants and competitions specifically for young entrepreneurs. These opportunities may provide financial support, mentorship, and exposure for their businesses.

Youth Entrepreneurship Programs
Look for youth entrepreneurship programs offered by local or national organizations. Some of these programs may provide funding, resources, and guidance to young entrepreneurs.

School Programs
Check if your child's school has entrepreneurship programs or initiatives that offer funding or support for student-led businesses. Some schools collaborate with local businesses or organizations to encourage entrepreneurship among students.

Crowdfunding
Platforms like Kickstarter or Indiegogo allow individuals, including young entrepreneurs, to raise funds for their projects. This involves presenting their business idea to a broader audience and encouraging people to contribute.

Parental Support
As a parent, you may consider providing financial support for your child's business endeavors. This could involve allocating a budget for their business activities, helping cover initial startup costs, or assisting with the purchase of necessary materials or equipment.

Family and Friends
Encourage your child to seek support from family and friends who may be willing to invest in or contribute to their business. This initial network can provide valuable financial assistance.

Local Business Competitions
Many communities organize business competitions that welcome young entrepreneurs. These competitions often come with cash prizes, mentorship opportunities, and exposure for the business.

Small Business Loans or Microfinance
Depending on the scale of the business, some local banks or microfinance institutions may offer small loans or financial assistance to young entrepreneurs. This option might be more applicable to older teenagers.

Local Business Competitions
Explore local community organizations, business associations, or chambers of commerce that may have programs to support youth entrepreneurship. They might offer funding or connect young entrepreneurs with local business sponsors.

Before pursuing any funding opportunities, it's important to research the eligibility criteria, application process, and any specific requirements associated with each option. Additionally, ensure that the financial support aligns with your child's age, business model, and the goals of their entrepreneurial venture.

It's raining cash!

Teen Biz Parent Guide

Should I get a bank loan or invest my 401k in my kid's business?

Investing your 401(k) or taking out a bank loan to fund your kid's business is a significant financial decision that requires careful consideration. Here are key factors to weigh before making such a commitment:

For Using Your 401(k)

Tax Implications
Withdrawals from a 401(k) before the age of 59½ are generally subject to income tax and a 10% early withdrawal penalty. Consider the tax implications of tapping into your retirement savings.

Impact on Retirement
Assess the potential impact on your long-term retirement savings. Withdrawing from your 401(k) could reduce the amount available for your retirement, affecting your financial well-being in the future.

Financial Consequences
Evaluate the financial consequences of using your 401(k) for a business investment. Ensure that the potential return on investment justifies the risk to your retirement savings.

Alternatives
Explore alternative funding options before resorting to using your 401(k). This could include seeking external investors, considering a business loan, or exploring grants and competitions for young entrepreneurs.

Legal and Financial Advice
Consult with a financial advisor or tax professional to understand the legal and financial implications of using your 401(k). They can provide personalized advice based on your specific situation.

For Taking a Bank Loan

Business Viability
Evaluate the viability of your kid's business. A thorough business plan outlining revenue projections, market analysis, and a clear business strategy is essential for securing a bank loan.

Creditworthiness
Consider your creditworthiness. A strong credit history is often a requirement for obtaining a business loan. Assess your credit scores and take steps to improve them if necessary.

Interest Rates and Terms
Compare interest rates and loan terms from different banks. Understand the total cost of the loan, including interest and fees. Choose a loan structure that aligns with your financial capabilities.

Repayment Plan
Develop a realistic repayment plan. Ensure that the business has the cash flow to cover loan repayments without jeopardizing its operations. A well-thought-out financial plan is crucial.

Collateral

Some loans may require collateral. Evaluate the assets that can be used as collateral and consider the risk associated with securing the loan against valuable assets.

Business Risk

Assess the overall risk associated with the business. Consider potential challenges and how the business will navigate them. Be realistic about the risks involved in repaying the loan.

Legal and Regulatory Compliance

Ensure that the business complies with all legal and regulatory requirements. Banks often require businesses to meet certain standards and adhere to legal guidelines.

Financial Expertise

If neither you nor your kid has significant financial expertise, consider seeking guidance from a financial advisor or accountant. They can help with financial planning, budgeting, and ensuring the business's financial health.

Loan Amount

Only borrow what is necessary for the business. Avoid taking on excessive debt that could strain the business's financial health.

Contingency Planning

Develop contingency plans in case the business faces unforeseen challenges. Consider how the business will manage repayments in the event of economic downturns or unexpected obstacles.

Before making any financial commitments, carefully weigh the potential benefits and risks. It's crucial to approach these decisions with a clear understanding of the financial implications and a well-thought-out plan for managing both personal and business finances. Consulting with financial professionals can provide valuable insights and help you make informed decisions.

When should I quit my job to go full time with my kid's business? Should I quit my job to go full time with my kid's business?

Deciding when to quit your job to go full-time with your kid's business is a significant and complex decision that requires careful consideration. Here are some factors to weigh before making this important choice:

Financial Stability

Assess your current financial situation. Ensure you have a financial safety net that can cover living expenses, healthcare, and any unexpected costs. Having savings in place provides a buffer as your kid's business may take time to generate a stable income.

Business Viability

Evaluate the viability and sustainability of your kid's business. Analyze key performance indicators, customer feedback, and financial projections. A solid business plan and evidence of market demand are crucial indicators of potential success.

Profitability and Cash Flow

Determine if the business is generating consistent profits and positive cash flow. It's important to have a clear understanding of the financial health of the business before relying on it as a primary income source.

Market Demand and Growth Potential

Assess the market demand for your kid's business and its growth potential. Consider the competitive landscape, target audience, and scalability. A business with strong growth prospects may be more promising for a full-time commitment.

Teen Biz Parent Guide

Business Plan and Strategy
Review the business plan and strategy. Ensure there is a well-defined plan for growth, marketing, and customer acquisition. A comprehensive strategy can provide confidence in the long-term success of the business.

Legal and Regulatory Considerations
Understand any legal or regulatory considerations associated with the business. Ensure compliance with local laws and regulations to avoid potential legal challenges that could impact the business's continuity.

Personal Risk Tolerance
Assess your personal risk tolerance. Understand that entrepreneurship involves inherent risks, and the transition from a stable job to entrepreneurship can be challenging. Consider how comfortable you are with uncertainty and potential financial fluctuations.

Support System
Discuss your decision with your family and ensure you have a support system in place. Communicate openly about the potential challenges and rewards of transitioning to full-time entrepreneurship with your kid's business.

Transition Plan
Develop a transition plan that outlines specific milestones and criteria for leaving your job. This plan could include financial goals, business performance metrics, and a timeline for making the transition.

Part-Time Commitment
Consider initially committing to the business on a part-time basis while maintaining your current job. This allows you to test the waters, assess the business's potential, and gradually transition to full-time entrepreneurship.

Professional Advice
Seek advice from mentors, business advisors, or financial professionals. They can provide valuable insights and perspectives on your specific situation, helping you make an informed decision.

Ultimately, the decision to quit your job and go full-time with your kid's business is highly personal and depends on various factors. It's important to strike a balance between pursuing your entrepreneurial aspirations and ensuring a stable financial foundation for you and your family. If possible, seek professional guidance and carefully plan the transition to mitigate risks and maximize the chances of success.

My kid wants to change their product or business. Now what?

When your child expresses a desire to change products or pivot the business, it's important to approach the situation with open communication and support. Here are steps to consider as a parent:

Initiate an Open Conversation
Have a candid and open conversation with your child. Encourage them to share the reasons behind wanting to change products or pivot the business. Actively listen to their ideas and concerns.

Understand the Motivation
Seek to understand the motivation behind the desire for change. It could be driven by market trends, personal interests, customer feedback, or a need to address challenges. Understanding the underlying reasons is crucial for providing meaningful support.

Assess Market Conditions
Collaboratively assess market conditions and industry trends. Research and discuss whether the proposed change aligns with current market demands and if it offers a viable and sustainable business opportunity.

Evaluate Learning Opportunities
Emphasize the learning opportunities associated with pivoting the business. Discuss how the experience of adapting to change, identifying new opportunities, and making strategic decisions contributes to their entrepreneurial development.

Encourage a Strategic Approach
Encourage your child to approach the change strategically. This may involve conducting market research, analyzing competitors, and developing a solid plan for implementing the changes. Help them understand the importance of thoughtful planning.

Financial Considerations
Discuss the financial implications of the change. Consider whether there are additional costs associated with the pivot and how these will be addressed. Ensure that your child has a realistic understanding of the financial aspects.

Support Decision-Making
Support your child in making informed decisions. Offer guidance and share your insights while empowering them to take ownership of the decision-making process. This fosters independence and resilience.

Encourage Flexibility
Reinforce the idea that entrepreneurship involves adaptation and flexibility. Changes in the business landscape are common, and being open to adjustments is a valuable skill for any entrepreneur.

Provide Resources
Offer resources and assistance as needed. This could include connecting them with mentors, providing access to educational materials, or assisting with networking opportunities. Ensure they have the support they need to navigate the change.

Celebrate Initiative
Celebrate your child's initiative and entrepreneurial spirit. Recognize the courage it takes to make a change and the commitment to continuous improvement. Positive reinforcement encourages a growth mindset.

Explore the New Direction Together
If appropriate, actively participate in exploring the new direction together. This could involve collaborative brainstorming sessions, researching potential suppliers, or assisting with the development of a revised business plan.

Reassure Emotional Support
Provide emotional support throughout the process. Changes in business direction can be both exciting and challenging. Reassure your child that you are there to support them, regardless of the outcome.

Remember that entrepreneurship involves adaptability and learning from experiences. Supporting your child through changes in their business not only fosters resilience but also helps them develop valuable skills for navigating the dynamic world of entrepreneurship.

Teen Biz Parent Guide

My kid wants to quit the business or doesn't like being an entrepreneur, what do I do?

If your child expresses a desire to quit the business or indicates that they do not enjoy being an entrepreneur, it's essential to approach the situation with understanding and support. Here are some steps to consider:

Open Communication
Initiate an open and honest conversation with your child. Encourage them to share their feelings, thoughts, and reasons for wanting to quit. Actively listen without judgment to gain a better understanding of their perspective.

Identify Concerns
Determine if some specific concerns or challenges are leading to their decision. It could be related to the nature of the business, personal stress, or a lack of interest. Identifying the root cause is crucial for addressing the issue effectively.

Explore Alternatives
Discuss potential alternatives or adjustments to the business that might make it more enjoyable for your child. This could involve changing certain aspects of the business model, exploring new ideas, or finding ways to align the business with their interests.

Reevaluate Expectations
Reevaluate the expectations surrounding the business. Ensure that the goals and aspirations align with your child's interests and capabilities. It's important not to place undue pressure on them to conform to a specific vision if it doesn't resonate with their passions.

Encourage Learning and Growth
Emphasize the value of the entrepreneurial experience as a learning opportunity, even if they decide to step back from the current business. Highlight the skills and insights gained through the entrepreneurial journey and how these can be applied in various aspects of life.

Consider Age and Developmental Stage
Take into account your child's age and developmental stage. Young entrepreneurs may need time to explore different interests and find their true passions. It's natural for interests to evolve as they grow.

Support Their Decision
If, after discussion, your child remains firm in their decision to quit the business, support their choice. Acknowledge their feelings and decisions, and reassure them that you are there to provide guidance and encouragement in whatever path they choose.

Reflect on the Experience
Encourage your child to reflect on their entrepreneurial experience. What did they enjoy? What did they learn? This reflection can help them gain insights into their interests and preferences for future endeavors.

Explore New Interests
Explore other activities or hobbies that might capture your child's interest. This could be an opportunity for them to discover new passions and talents.

Encourage a Positive Mindset
Foster a positive mindset by emphasizing that it's okay to explore different paths and that the entrepreneurial journey is just one aspect of their life. Reinforce the idea that personal happiness and fulfillment are essential.

Remember that the decision to be an entrepreneur should be driven by genuine interest and passion. Supporting your child's choices, even if they differ from your initial expectations, contributes to their overall well-being and encourages a healthy approach to decision-making and personal growth.

How do I reward my kid without making entrepreneurship too easy?

Rewarding your child for their entrepreneurial efforts is important, but it's equally crucial to ensure that they continue to face challenges and grow. Here's how you can reward your child without making entrepreneurship too easy:

Recognition and Praise
Offer genuine recognition and praise for specific achievements and milestones. Highlight their hard work, creativity, and dedication in their entrepreneurial journey.

Celebratory Events
Plan celebratory events or gatherings to mark significant milestones in the business. This could include a small party, a family dinner, or a special outing to acknowledge their accomplishments.

Educational Opportunities
Invest in educational opportunities related to entrepreneurship. Enroll them in workshops, courses, or programs that can enhance their business knowledge and skills.

Networking Opportunities
Facilitate networking opportunities with experienced entrepreneurs, mentors, or professionals in the field. Building connections can provide valuable insights and open doors to new possibilities.

Business Development Resources
Provide resources to support the development of their business. This could involve investing in upgraded equipment, software, or tools that can contribute to the business's growth.

Business Coaching or Mentorship
Arrange for business coaching or mentorship from experienced entrepreneurs. Having a mentor can offer guidance, advice, and a sounding board for their ideas.

Financial Literacy Lessons
Offer financial literacy lessons or experiences. Help them understand budgeting, profit margins, and financial management. This knowledge is valuable for both business and personal finance.

Customized Business Gear
Design or purchase customized business gear, such as branded merchandise or personalized items related to their business. This creates a sense of pride and professionalism.

Learning Experiences
Reward them with unique learning experiences. This could involve attending industry conferences, visiting successful businesses, or participating in events that expose them to different aspects of entrepreneurship.

Collaborative Projects
Engage in collaborative projects together. This could be a joint venture or a shared activity related to the business. Working together strengthens your connection and provides an opportunity to share insights.

Access to Entrepreneurial Networks
Grant them access to entrepreneurial networks or communities. This exposure can broaden their perspectives and offer a platform for collaboration with other young entrepreneurs.

Encourage Philanthropy
Foster a sense of social responsibility by encouraging philanthropy. Allocate a portion of the business's profits to a charitable cause or engage in community service projects.

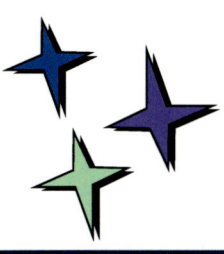

Internship or Job Shadowing
Arrange for internship opportunities or job shadowing experiences with professionals in their industry. Practical exposure can provide valuable insights and inspiration.

Remember to tailor the rewards to your child's individual preferences and interests. The key is to balance recognition with opportunities for growth, ensuring that the rewards contribute to their continued development as an entrepreneur.

What are the Taxes and Legal implications of my kid starting a business?

Legal Implications

Business Structure
The choice of business structure (e.g., sole proprietorship, partnership, LLC) affects legal implications. Each structure has different levels of personal liability, taxation, and regulatory requirements.

Business Name Registration
Depending on your location, your child may need to register the business name. This ensures that the chosen name is not already in use and complies with local regulations.

Permits and Licenses
Check if there are specific permits or licenses required for the type of business your child is starting. This varies by industry and location.

Age Restrictions
Be aware of any age restrictions or requirements for young entrepreneurs in your jurisdiction. Some places may have regulations regarding the legal age for certain business activities.

Contracts and Agreements
If the business involves agreements or contracts, ensure that they are legally sound. Consider consulting with a legal professional to draft or review any documents.

Tax Implications

Tax Identification Number (TIN)
Obtain a Tax Identification Number (TIN) for the business. This is used for tax purposes and may be required for opening a business bank account.

Income Reporting
Your child will need to report business income on their tax return. Keep detailed records of all income and expenses related to the business.

Self-Employment Taxes
If the business generates income, your child may be subject to self-employment taxes. These taxes cover Social Security and Medicare contributions.

Record Keeping
Maintain thorough and accurate records of all financial transactions related to the business. This includes invoices, receipts, and any other financial documentation.

Self-Employment Taxes
If the business generates income, your child may be subject to self-employment taxes. These taxes cover Social Security and Medicare contributions.

Record Keeping
Maintain thorough and accurate records of all financial transactions related to the business. This includes invoices, receipts, and any other financial documentation.

Deductions and Credits
Explore potential tax deductions and credits available to small businesses. This may include deductions for business expenses, equipment, or educational expenses related to the business.

Sales Tax
If the business involves selling products or services, check if there are sales tax obligations. In some jurisdictions, businesses need to collect and remit sales tax to the appropriate authorities.

Employment Taxes
If the business hires employees, be aware of employment tax obligations. This includes withholding income tax and Social Security contributions.

Consult a Tax Professional
Given the unique circumstances of a kid entrepreneur, consulting with a tax professional is advisable. They can provide personalized advice based on your child's specific business activities and circumstances.

State and Local Taxes
Understand state and local tax obligations. Some areas may have additional taxes or regulations that apply to businesses operating within their jurisdiction.

Tax Deadlines
Familiarize yourself and your child with tax filing deadlines. Missing deadlines can result in penalties or interest charges.

It's crucial to consult with legal and tax professionals to ensure compliance with all applicable laws and regulations. They can provide tailored advice based on your specific location and the nature of the business. Additionally, staying informed about changes in tax laws and regulations is essential for ongoing compliance.

"As Ben Franklin once wrote, "...in this world, nothing can be said to be certain, except death and taxes.""

Teen Biz Parent Guide

What are business entities?

Business entities refer to the legal structures that individuals or groups use to organize, operate, and manage their businesses. Choosing the right business entity is a crucial decision as it affects various aspects, including liability, taxation, management, and compliance requirements. Here are common types of business entities:

Sole Proprietorship

A sole proprietorship is the simplest form of business entity, where a single individual owns and operates the business. The owner is personally responsible for all aspects of the business, including debts and liabilities.

Partnership

A partnership involves two or more individuals who agree to share profits and losses in a business. There are two main types: general partnerships (where all partners have equal responsibility) and limited partnerships (where one or more partners have limited liability).

Limited Liability Company (LLC)

An LLC is a flexible business structure that combines elements of a corporation and a partnership. It provides limited liability protection to its owners (called members) and allows for pass-through taxation, where profits and losses are reported on the members' individual tax returns.

Corporation

A corporation is a separate legal entity owned by shareholders. It offers limited liability protection to shareholders, meaning their personal assets are generally protected from business debts. Corporations can be classified as C corporations or S corporations, each with different tax implications.

S Corporation

An S corporation is a specific type of corporation that elects to pass corporate income, deductions, and credits through to its shareholders for federal tax purposes. It combines the limited liability advantages of a corporation with the pass-through taxation of a partnership.

Nonprofit Organization

Nonprofit organizations are formed for purposes other than making a profit. They can take various legal structures, such as nonprofit corporations or charitable trusts, and are typically exempt from paying income taxes.

Cooperative

A cooperative is a business owned and operated by its members. Members, who can be customers, employees, or producers, jointly own the business and share in its profits or benefits.

Professional Corporation (PC) or Limited Liability Partnership (LLP)

Professionals like doctors, lawyers, and accountants often choose a professional corporation (PC) or limited liability partnership (LLP) as their business entity. These structures provide liability protection while allowing professionals to practice their respective trades.

Choosing the right business entity depends on factors such as the nature of the business, the number of owners, liability concerns, tax implications, and management preferences. It's advisable to consult with legal and financial professionals to determine the most suitable structure for a particular business.

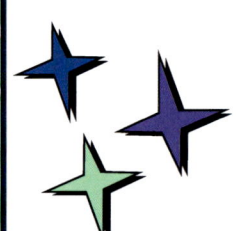

When to file an LLC (hint, hint: not at the beginning)

Deciding when to file for an LLC (Limited Liability Company) or corporation for your kid's business involves considering several factors. Here are some key considerations to help guide your decision:

Business Complexity

If the business is relatively simple, with a single owner and straightforward operations, starting as a sole proprietorship or partnership might be suitable initially. As the business grows or evolves, transitioning to an LLC or corporation can be considered.

Liability Protection

If one of your primary concerns is protecting your child's personal assets from business debts and liabilities, forming an LLC or corporation is advisable. These structures offer limited liability, meaning personal assets are generally shielded from business-related obligations.

Long-Term Viability

Consider the long-term viability and growth potential of the business. If you envision significant expansion, seeking investors, or transferring ownership in the future, a corporation might be a more suitable choice due to its scalability and ability to issue shares.

Tax Considerations

Evaluate the tax implications of different business structures. LLCs and S corporations offer pass-through taxation, where business profits and losses flow through to the owners' personal tax returns. C corporations have a separate tax entity, potentially subject to double taxation.

Ownership Structure

Consider the ownership structure of the business. If there are multiple owners or a desire to have different classes of ownership (such as voting and non-voting shares), a corporation may provide more flexibility in structuring ownership.

Investment and Funding

If your child plans to seek investment or funding from external sources, such as investors or venture capitalists, a corporation is often more attractive. Corporations can issue stock, making it easier to attract investors.

Formalities and Compliance

Corporations typically have more formalities and compliance requirements than LLCs. Consider the administrative burden and whether your child is prepared to meet the additional record-keeping and reporting obligations associated with a corporation.

Professional Advice

Consult with legal and financial professionals. They can provide personalized advice based on your child's specific business goals, structure, and legal and regulatory requirements in your jurisdiction.

Business Name and Branding

Check the availability of the desired business name and consider how it aligns with your child's branding strategy. Some names might be more suitable for certain business structures.

Transition Timing

If the decision is to start with a simpler structure (e.g., sole proprietorship or partnership) initially, plan for a potential transition to an LLC or corporation as the business grows or faces changing circumstances.

Keep in mind that the specific rules and regulations for forming and operating businesses vary by jurisdiction. Therefore, it's essential to research the requirements and comply with local laws when establishing the business entity. Consulting with professionals can help ensure that the chosen structure aligns with your child's business objectives and provides the desired legal and financial benefits.

Teen Biz Parent Guide

What are the labor laws associated with kids under 16 working or running a business?

Labor laws for kids under 16 working or running a business vary by jurisdiction and are designed to protect young individuals by ensuring a balance between work and education. Below are some general principles, but it's crucial to consult with local labor authorities or legal professionals to understand specific regulations in your area:

General Principles

Minimum Age for Employment
Most jurisdictions have a minimum age for employment, typically around 14 or 16. This age may vary, so it's essential to check local laws.

Restricted Working Hours
Labor laws often specify restricted working hours for young individuals during school days to prevent excessive interference with education.

Limit on Hours per Day
There is usually a limit on the number of hours a young person can work per day, including weekends, to prevent overworking.

Prohibited Occupations
Certain hazardous occupations are prohibited for individuals under a certain age to protect their safety.

Work Permits
Some jurisdictions require young individuals to obtain a work permit to engage in employment, often issued by school authorities.

School Attendance
Labor laws prioritize school attendance, requiring young individuals to attend school regularly.

Parental Consent
Parental consent may be required for young individuals to work, with parents or legal guardians acknowledging their awareness and approval of their child's employment.

Running a Business

Entrepreneurial Activities
Entrepreneurial pursuits such as starting a small business or engaging in self-employment are often encouraged for young individuals.

Parental Involvement
Parents play a crucial role in supporting and overseeing their child's entrepreneurial activities, handling legal aspects, and ensuring compliance with regulations.

Safety Considerations
Parents must ensure that the business activities are age-appropriate and do not pose risks to the child's well-being.

Educational Balance
Maintaining a balance between entrepreneurial pursuits and education is essential to ensure that the child's academic responsibilities are not compromised.

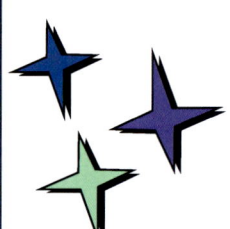
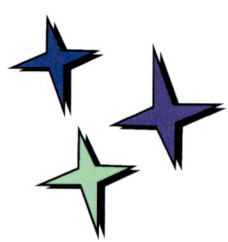

Compliance with Business Laws
Any business run by a minor must comply with local business laws and regulations, including registration, tax obligations, and industry-specific rules.

Limitations on Financial Transactions
Depending on the jurisdiction, there may be limitations on minors entering into contracts or engaging in certain financial transactions, requiring parental assistance.

Always check with local labor authorities, child labor offices, or legal professionals to ensure compliance with specific laws and regulations governing young individuals working or running a business in your area. It's crucial to prioritize the well-being, education, and safety of the child while encouraging their entrepreneurial spirit within the bounds of the law.

How do I prepare taxes with my kid's business?

Preparing taxes for your kid's business involves several steps to ensure accurate reporting and compliance with tax regulations. Here is a general guide to help you navigate the process:

Keep Detailed Records
Maintain thorough and organized records of all income and expenses related to the business. This includes sales receipts, invoices, receipts for business expenses, and any relevant financial documents.

Determine the Business Structure
Identify the legal structure of the business, whether it's a sole proprietorship, partnership, LLC, or corporation. Different structures have varying tax implications.

Obtain a Tax Identification Number (TIN)
Ensure that the business has a Tax Identification Number (TIN). This is necessary for tax reporting purposes and may be required for opening a business bank account.

Choose the Appropriate Tax Form
Depending on the business structure, choose the appropriate tax form for filing. Common forms include:
Sole Proprietorship: Use Schedule C or Schedule C-EZ (Form 1040).
Partnership: File Form 1065, U.S. Return of Partnership Income.
LLC: Depending on how the LLC is taxed, it may use the same forms as a sole proprietorship or partnership, or it may elect to be treated as a corporation.
Corporation: File Form 1120, U.S. Corporation Income Tax Return.

Report Business Income
Report all business income on the appropriate tax form. This includes income from sales, services, or any other sources related to the business.

Deduct Business Expenses
Deduct eligible business expenses to reduce the taxable income. Common deductible expenses include rent, utilities, supplies, and other costs directly related to the business.

Depreciation
If the business owns assets with a useful life longer than one year (e.g., equipment, computers), consider depreciation deductions. This allows the cost of the asset to be spread over its useful life.

Self-Employment Taxes
If the business owner is subject to self-employment taxes, ensure that these taxes are calculated and reported accurately. Self-employment taxes cover Social Security and Medicare contributions.

Business Tax Credits

Explore potential business tax credits that may apply. These can help reduce the overall tax liability. Common credits include those related to research and development, energy efficiency, or hiring certain employees.

State and Local Taxes

Be aware of state and local tax obligations. Depending on the location, there may be additional taxes or requirements for the business.

Seek Professional Assistance

Given the complexity of tax regulations, consider seeking professional assistance from a certified public accountant (CPA) or tax professional. They can provide tailored advice, ensure compliance, and help maximize deductions.

File Timely

Ensure that tax returns are filed by the deadline. Failing to file on time may result in penalties and interest.

Keep Personal and Business Finances Separate

Maintain separate bank accounts for personal and business finances. This separation makes it easier to track business transactions and ensures accurate reporting.

Monitor Changes in Tax Laws

Stay informed about changes in tax laws that may affect the business. Tax regulations can evolve, and staying updated helps in adapting to any new requirements or opportunities.

Remember that tax requirements may vary based on the business structure, location, and specific circumstances. It's advisable to consult with a tax professional to ensure accurate and compliant tax preparation for your kid's business.

How can I reduce my tax liability?

Reducing your tax liability when you have a job and your kid has a business involves strategic financial planning and taking advantage of available tax deductions and credits. Here are several strategies to consider:

Claim Dependent Child Deductions

If your child is your dependent, you may be eligible for various tax deductions, including the Child Tax Credit, which can reduce your overall tax liability.

Invest in Education Savings

Contribute to tax-advantaged education savings accounts, such as a 529 plan. Funds from these accounts can be used for your child's education expenses, and contributions may be deductible at the state level.

Employ Your Child in the Family Business

If your child is involved in the family business, consider employing them. This allows you to shift income to your child, potentially at a lower tax rate. Ensure that the compensation is reasonable for the services provided.

Deduct Business Expenses

If you financially support your child's business, you may be able to deduct certain expenses related to the business. Ensure that these expenses are legitimate and necessary for the business operations.

Contribute to Retirement Accounts

Contribute to tax-advantaged retirement accounts, such as a 401(k) or IRA. These contributions can reduce your taxable income. Additionally, consider establishing a retirement plan for the family business.

Take Advantage of Flexible Spending Accounts (FSAs) or Health Savings Accounts (HSAs)

Contribute to FSAs or HSAs to cover eligible medical expenses. These contributions are often tax-deductible and can help lower your overall tax liability.

Explore Tax Credits

Investigate available tax credits, such as the Child and Dependent Care Credit or the American Opportunity Credit for education expenses. These credits can directly reduce your tax liability.

Gift Assets Strategically

If you plan to transfer assets to your child, consider doing so strategically to take advantage of gift tax exclusions. Consulting with a tax professional can help optimize this process.

Leverage Business Tax Planning

If you own a business, work with a tax professional to implement effective tax planning strategies. This may include optimizing deductions, credits, and taking advantage of favorable business tax provisions.

Maximize Itemized Deductions

Explore opportunities to maximize your itemized deductions. This includes deductions for mortgage interest, property taxes, charitable contributions, and medical expenses.

Consider Tax-Efficient Investments

Invest in tax-efficient funds or investment strategies that may reduce your overall tax liability. Consult with a financial advisor to explore tax-efficient investment options.

Stay Informed About Tax Law Changes

Regularly stay informed about changes in tax laws. Understanding new regulations can help you adjust your financial strategies to minimize tax liability.

Hire a Tax Professional

Engage the services of a tax professional or CPA to ensure that you are taking advantage of all available tax-saving opportunities. A tax professional can provide personalized advice based on your specific financial situation.

Remember that tax planning should be approached holistically, considering both your employment income and any income or deductions associated with your child's business. It's advisable to seek professional advice to develop a comprehensive tax strategy tailored to your family's specific circumstances.

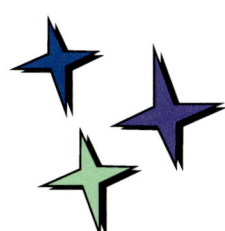

How do we separate my personal taxes from the business taxes?

Establish Separate Bank Accounts

- **Personal Account**: Maintain a personal bank account for your individual income, expenses, and personal financial transactions.

- **Business Account**: Open a separate business bank account for your kid's business to handle all business-related income and expenses.

Obtain Individual and Business Tax Identification Numbers

- **Individual Tax ID (SSN):** Use your Social Security Number (SSN) for your personal tax filings.

- **Business Tax ID (EIN or SSN):** Obtain a separate Employer Identification Number (EIN) for your kid's business, or use their SSN depending on the business structure.

Maintain Separate Financial Records

- **Personal Finances:** Keep detailed records of your personal income, expenses, and deductions.

- **Business Finances:** Maintain thorough records for your kid's business, including income, expenses, receipts, and financial documentation.

File Separate Tax Returns

- **Personal Tax Return:** File your personal tax return using the appropriate forms, reporting all personal income, deductions, and credits.

- **Business Tax Return:** File a separate tax return for your kid's business, reporting business income, expenses, and relevant details based on its structure.

Use Different Accounting Software

- **Personal Finances:** Utilize accounting software or systems for tracking personal finances.

- **Business Finances:** Implement separate accounting software for managing the kid's business finances to ensure accurate bookkeeping and financial reporting.

Clearly Define Business Expenses

Clearly identify and document business expenses separately from personal expenses for accurate tax reporting and deductions.

Consult with Tax Professionals

Engage tax professionals, such as accountants or CPAs, to ensure compliance with both personal and business tax obligations and receive personalized advice.

Understand Business Structure Implications

Different business structures have varying implications for personal liability and tax obligations. Understand the specific requirements associated with your kid's business structure.

Stay Informed on Tax Laws

Regularly update your knowledge of tax laws and regulations to adapt to any new requirements or opportunities.

Monitor Financial Transactions

Regularly monitor financial transactions in both personal and business accounts to ensure accuracy and streamline the tax preparation process.

By following these steps and maintaining a clear separation between personal and business finances, you can streamline tax reporting, reduce the risk of errors, and ensure compliance with both personal and business tax obligations. If in doubt, seek advice from tax professionals who can provide guidance tailored to your specific situation.

How to Set Up a Trust Fund with the Proceeds from Their Business

Setting up a trust fund for your kid with the proceeds from their business involves several steps. It's important to work with legal and financial professionals to ensure that the trust is structured appropriately and complies with relevant laws. Here is a general guide:

Define Objectives

Clearly outline the objectives of the trust fund. Consider the purpose, the intended benefits for your child, and any specific conditions or restrictions.

Choose a Trust Type

Select the type of trust that aligns with your goals. Common types include:
- Revocable Living Trust: This can be altered during the grantor's lifetime.
- Irrevocable Trust: Generally, cannot be modified or revoked once established.
- Testamentary Trust: Created through a will and becomes effective after the grantor's death.

Appoint a Trustee
Designate a trustee responsible for managing and distributing the trust assets. This can be an individual, a professional trustee, or a financial institution.

Determine Funding Mechanism
Decide how the trust will be funded. In this case, it would involve allocating a portion of the proceeds from your kid's business to the trust.

Establish Legal Framework
Work with an attorney to draft the necessary legal documents, including the trust agreement. Clearly articulate the terms, conditions, and responsibilities of the trust.

Name the Trust
Choose a name for the trust that reflects its purpose or your kid's business legacy.

Specify Beneficiaries
Clearly identify your child as the primary beneficiary. You may also outline provisions for secondary beneficiaries or contingent beneficiaries.

Set Distribution Guidelines
Define the guidelines for distributing trust assets to your child. This could include specific milestones, age-based distributions, or educational achievements.

Consider Tax Implications
Consult with tax professionals to understand the tax implications of the trust. Different types of trusts may have varying tax consequences.

Address Contingencies
Plan for contingencies, such as what happens if the primary beneficiary predeceases you or if circumstances change.

Plan for Succession
Consider the succession of trustees in case the appointed trustee is unable or unwilling to fulfill their duties.

Comply with Local Laws
Ensure that the trust complies with local laws and regulations. Legal requirements may vary depending on your jurisdiction.

Fund the Trust
Transfer the designated portion of the proceeds from your kid's business into the trust. This may involve retitling assets or updating beneficiary designations.

Educate Trustees and Beneficiaries
If your child is old enough, educate them about the trust and its purpose. Ensure that trustees understand their responsibilities.

Regular Review
Periodically review the trust terms to ensure they remain aligned with your intentions. Update the trust if necessary due to changes in circumstances, laws, or family dynamics.

Communicate
Communicate with relevant parties, including your child, about the existence and purpose of the trust. Transparency can help avoid misunderstandings.

Maintain Records
Keep detailed records of trust-related transactions and decisions. Good record-keeping is essential for transparency and compliance.

Seek Professional Advice
Consult with legal and financial professionals throughout the process to ensure that the trust is established correctly and fulfills your objectives.

Establishing a trust fund is a complex legal process, and seeking professional guidance is crucial. By carefully planning and executing the steps outlined above, you can create a trust fund that provides financial security and support for your child based on the proceeds from their business.

How do we build a family legacy together?

Building a family legacy through your kid's business or entrepreneurial endeavors involves creating a lasting impact that transcends generations. Here are steps to help you establish and nurture a family legacy:

Define Your Values and Vision
Clearly articulate the values that are important to your family. Define a vision that aligns with these values and represents the legacy you want to leave.

Incorporate Family Values into the Business
Ensure that the kid's business reflects and embodies the family values. This could be evident in the company culture, mission statement, and business practices.

Promote a Strong Work Ethic
Instill a strong work ethic in your child from an early age. Teach the importance of hard work, dedication, and perseverance, which are key elements of a successful entrepreneurial journey.

Encourage Entrepreneurial Mindset
Foster an entrepreneurial mindset by encouraging creativity, problem-solving, and a willingness to take calculated risks. This mindset can extend beyond the business to various aspects of life.

Establish a Family Business Structure
If applicable, consider structuring the business as a family-owned enterprise. This can involve formalizing roles, responsibilities, and succession plans within the family.

Educate and Mentor
Actively engage in educating and mentoring your child in both business and life skills. Share your experiences, provide guidance, and help them develop a holistic understanding of entrepreneurship.

Document Family Stories and Achievements
Document the family's entrepreneurial journey, achievements, and challenges. This can include keeping a family journal, creating a website, or producing videos that capture important moments.

Create Traditions and Rituals
Establish traditions and rituals associated with the business. This could include annual family meetings, celebrating business milestones together, or creating unique family traditions linked to entrepreneurial achievements.

Involve Multiple Generations
If possible, involve multiple generations in the business. This allows the transfer of knowledge, skills, and values from one generation to the next, creating a sense of continuity.

Cultivate Philanthropy
Embed philanthropy into the family legacy by giving back to the community or supporting charitable causes. This creates a positive impact beyond the business realm.

Teen Biz Parent Guide

Focus on Sustainability
Build a business model that emphasizes sustainability, not only in terms of environmental impact but also regarding the long-term viability and success of the enterprise.

Celebrate Family Achievements
Celebrate not only business achievements but also personal milestones and accomplishments of family members. Acknowledge and appreciate each member's contributions.

Encourage Continued Education
Support ongoing education and professional development within the family. This ensures that family members stay updated on industry trends and new opportunities.

Establish Family Governance
Consider establishing family governance structures to manage business-related decisions and succession planning. This can include family councils or boards.

Embrace Adaptability
Recognize the importance of adaptability in the business and family legacy. Embrace change, innovation, and the ability to evolve with the times.

Document Succession Plans
Develop clear succession plans for the business. This includes defining roles for future generations and ensuring a smooth transition of leadership.

Encourage Family Members to Pursue Their Passions
Support family members in pursuing their individual passions and entrepreneurial endeavors. A diverse range of interests can contribute to a rich family legacy.

Maintain Strong Communication
Foster open and honest communication within the family. Regularly discuss the business, values, and vision for the family legacy.

Preserve Family Traditions
Preserve and pass down family traditions that contribute to the unique identity of your family legacy.

Seek Professional Advice
Consult with professionals, such as family business consultants or advisors, to navigate complex issues related to family dynamics, succession planning, and governance.

Building a family legacy through your kid's business requires intentionality, a long-term perspective, and a commitment to shared values. By incorporating these principles, you can create a meaningful and enduring legacy that spans generations.

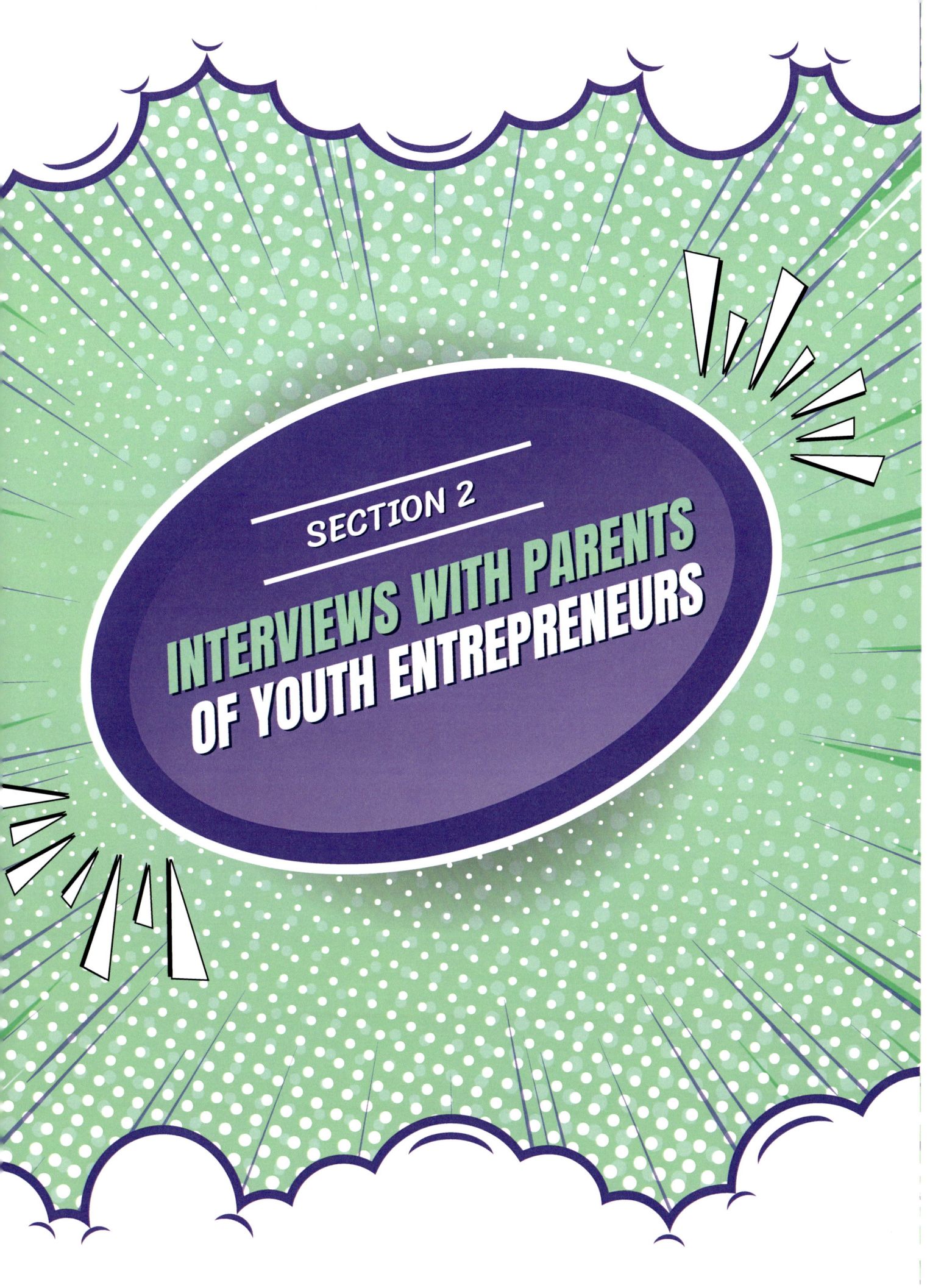

Teen Biz Parent Guide

INTERVIEW WITH CHRISTY MANNERING MOTHER OF BRAEDEN MANNERING

About Braeden Mannering and Brae's Brown Bags ("3B)

The mission of Brae's Brown Bags is to provide healthy snacks to homeless and low-income individuals. Every bag includes a letter from Braeden, contact information for additional services who can provide further assistance, three healthy snacks (each one is below 180 calories), and a bottle of water.

Brae's Brown Bags has given Braeden a platform to speak about food insecurity, homelessness and poverty at schools, conferences and legislative sessions. In September 2015, he launched 3B Ripples, which helps schools and youth organizations to launch their own 3B student chapters in their local communities.

Our belief is that every person regardless of their financial situation deserves to have access to healthy food. This helps to balance the paradox between obesity and food insecurity.

What started as one brown bag branched off into multiple important directions including: three specialty bags, giving talks to groups about food insecurity with a special interest in talking with youth at schools and youth-based organizations about food insecurity and public service. 3B also raises money to help other hunger relief organizations.

Brae's Brown Bags provide hope and nourishment to each person who receives one.

Christy, tell us a little bit about you, Brayden, and this incredible business.

My name is Christine Mannering, and my son's name is Braeden. When he was 9 years old, he started Brae's Brown Bags. He has a mission of fighting hunger, and his goal is to ensure we get healthy food options out to low-income populations around Delaware, which has extended across the country. He works in these populations, with shelters, kitchens, and schools, and also to raise awareness and educate other young people that food insecurity is an issue and they can help fix the problem.

Teen Biz Parent Guide

How did he become interested in entrepreneurship or being an entrepreneur?

Braeden was interested in social good. Former First Lady Michelle Obama encouraged Braeden to think about ways to pay it forward. He won a food competition called the "Healthy Lunchtime Challenge" when he was 9 years old, and we had incredible luck being at the same table as Michelle Obama. She talked about eating healthy and living a healthy lifestyle, which was really important. She spoke to kids from every state of the country. It was a kid's State dinner, and Brayden represented Delaware.

She told him this was an excellent opportunity for him to think about how he could pay it forward. He didn't really understand that. Washington, DC, has a very high homeless population, and he asked questions like "why people were asking for money?" and "Why were they sitting at the train station"? He wanted to give his souvenir money away.

We saw a homeless person with a sign on the street in Delaware right near where we live. I was driving, and I have two other younger kids. When we got home, Brayden went into the kitchen and was packing food, and he said Mom, I want to take this food to the person we saw. I want to do what Michelle Obama asked me to do. In his 9-year-old mind, he took her decision to want people to have a healthy lifestyle and his desire to help people, and he merged them, which became Brae's Brown Bags. And it took off because it was so simple he could tell his friends about it. Somehow, it got back to the White House, and they invited him back! Because of that, he could see that sharing that story with other young people made them want to get involved.

I told him, why don't we think about what Michelle Obama asks of you and about how we can pay it forward and find a way to help these people without giving away money because we don't have more money to give them.

What challenges have you and Braeden struggled with?

Healthy food is expensive. When you're working with soup kitchens and shelters, they prefer non-perishable food, so finding healthy supplies that are affordable is really difficult. Another challenge was school, family, and work balance. He was young when he started, and the teachers and principal were open to working with him. But as he got older, it became a little bit harder because his academic demands increased. There would be instances where he would get invited to talk somewhere and it was an unexcused absence since the school wouldn't approve it. From then, it was up to me to say "Okay, his grades are good. He can handle missing this one day," or having to turn down an invite.

When we went through COVID, a lot of our work - which was mainly in public schools - got shut down and we are still struggling to get back into schools. Which, understandably so, since school protocols have changed and Braeden's in college now, so his classes are during the day.

There's been a number of challenges one after another, and one that was harder for me to understand was that he didn't want to be a superstar. He wanted to be Braeden. He wanted to be the kid who played video games and rode on his scooter. It was hard for him to have that limelight sometimes, but he's been given so many opportunities to attend different events - like meeting Gwen Stefani at the Disney Radio Music Awards in Los Angeles. As his mom, I want to protect him and I want him to have a happy life, but I also see that this is important to him and has become important to all of us. This includes the community, which was another challenge since people knew where we lived.

People would leave toiletry items and we would come home to see that - which was a good thing, but we needed a storage unit since we lived in a townhome. Fortunately, I lived close to family and my parents, who opened their basement to become our Brae's Brown Bags storage area. Again, we did not anticipate how this would take off and also had ignorance to the problem. I learned that, just in Braeden's school district, there were over 700 homeless families. I've been privileged to always have food on the table, so that was a challenge too, when places we knew of - like the woods and other areas - people would be out in 18 degrees. There was one time where we drove four people who were sitting outside at an unopened shelter. They asked us to take them home and we drove them to the woods.

I cried the whole way home because when you immerse yourself in that environment, you realize you can only help so little. We put our contact information in these brown bags containing healthy food with bottles of water, and gave them to shelters or soup kitchens where they can get help. But, even then, they ask us to leave them in the woods. Everything was very hard to breathe in, but the concepts that he had to learn at such a young age have really impacted many including myself, so there have been many challenges.

Getting him involved in leadership was also important to me, so I connected him with the Jefferson Awards in their Lead 360 program. This helped us get connected to other like-minded people across the country, including many youth leadership conferences and schools. Once I could connect with them, they would invite Brayden to talk and I made sure to get my background checks and things alike since I was obviously an adult. So, it's just learning all those intricacies to enjoy putting my best foot forward in order to get Brayden through the doors. It still is hard to filter emails and phone calls - and it was much harder in the beginning - but he can do a lot of that now on his own.

As a parent, how do you support your child in their entrepreneurial endeavors?

The scheduler, the transporter, the grant writer - I learned all of those things. It was hard to know what grants to qualify for because, as I said, one of the challenges is the expense of supplies - in particular non-perishable healthy food. We started with a website called "Start-a-Snowball," and they gave us our first $100 grant. They also connected us with other organizations that work with you to make positive changes in the world. So, for me, definitely keeping a record of our finances and filling out the 990-N form for tax purposes. We always made under 50,000 a year by a landslide, so we never had to do expensive tax preparation. It was a lot of networking, and once people met Braeden, I didn't have to do much at all. He's always been the heart and the voice of Brae's Brown Bags - I just scheduled the appearances. I also did a lot with legislative calls because I knew that, if I could get Braeden in front of the right people, he would get more support from the state. So, I definitely helped with the finances, networking, scheduling, driving, sending emails to companies like Welch's fruit snacks to ask for snacks for our bags, and I would see what other grant or funding opportunities will be available.

How do you balance your child's entrepreneurial activities with their academic and social life?

I will say, it was easier when he was younger because I was controlling it more due to him being little and not having after school activities. Once he got into middle school, he was part of the BPA (Business Professionals of America), wanted to spend time with friends, including high school, but COVID hit. I just had to be present in what was happening. He came home and if life was not treating him right that day, we wouldn't talk about Brae's Brown Bags. I would let people know that Brayden was off the clock. If there was an emergency shelter opening for bad weather, I would handle it. Whenever anyone wants to take a photo, want him to respond to an email, or want him to talk, I always ask him if he's comfortable. He's really good at saying no and that he's not into it right now, and I appreciate him for being honest. It wouldn't be something he would love if I were to push him. I also have to come outside of myself like "Christy, you're 43. Your life experiences have been so great. He is eight - remember what you were like when you were that age." But, again, being a single parent and having two younger siblings, Braeden and I's relationships relies on raw, transparent honesty. It doesn't matter if it's going to hurt my feelings - I gotta know what you're feeling right now and I just have to own that. That is number one, I always have to make sure I'm asking him how he's feeling, if it's comfortable for him, and listen.

Are there specific skills or lessons your child has learned through entrepreneurship?

Braeden has taught me how to be a public speaker. It;'s not something I was ever comfortable with before since I was a web developer and liked working behind the scenes. If anything, I think the roles are reversed since he taught me. But, one of the things that I had to help him with was being more concise - like an elevator pitch. Another would be empathy because a lot of times you can see people strung out or going through withdrawal. When we would work in colder temperatures, hypothermia sets in really quickly. There would also be people who looked drunk but weren't, and in fact couldn't walk. He needed to learn to "poker face it". You never want to be fake to people, but you also don't want to be judgemental since it's very easy to judge with things you may not understand. You need to be compassionate and genuine, and realize that everybody is on a different journey that you may not see. So I think emotional intelligence is a skill he got to learn at a young age and he has carried that forward. He is one of the calmest, young people I know that can handle mental health and high tense issues and be able to hone it in.

Have you seen any positive changes in your child's confidence or leadership skills since starting their business?

It's easy for me to see the changes now that he's 20 years old. He's a completely different person than when he was a little kid, but as a child, his leadership skills were incredible. He would be in charge of a room of 400 kids - grabbing the microphone, jumping down the stage, and be in the middle of them and talk. He was talking to his peers, he knew they would listen to him and knew that they would be excited about what he was talking about. But, the leadership aspect of it, he wanted to create more leaders. It was never about "Let's see how many people I can get to follow me," and I feel like there's a lot of young people these days that are all about followers. Social media has kind of forced that upon everybody, but Braeden was never about that. He was all about the ripple effect of sharing a story and watching people run with it - whether they wanted to help with food insecurity, shelter animals, or help recycle. He loves seeing them become leaders, and he has so many friends now around the country because they just lifted each other up.

How has the experience been with him teaching his friends and encouraging entrepreneurship?

One thing Braeden made very clear was that he never wanted to be a speaker for whatever class he was currently in. So, he has gone back to his schools and talked, but while he was in middle school, he did not. He separated his personal life in that way from his 3B light. I respected his decision and like I said, he just wanted to be Brayden to those people. It was a little tricky since the schools did want to hear from him, but I didn't want to take that world away from him where he could just be himself. He doesn't talk about it as "You can start this," he doesn't use the word entrepreneur. He uses the word "change maker," "Bro," and says "if this bothers you, go be the change." He did start 3B Ripples, which were student chapters. So, we would provide a bit of funding if the school needed it, and they would build an application to see how many students were interested. We would provide a starter kit, he would talk with the students, and then they became their own chapter. We had a reporting form they could fill out and say where they took the bags, like taking them to a church or soup kitchen. Working with the 3D Ripples, I think it was a neat idea. I came up with the "3D Ripples," but he likes describing that to young people. I think it's actually more fun for him now as a twenty year old to talk to seven year olds, where he gets down on the tiny chairs and explains the ripples from throwing a little rock into the water. He's so calm and chill that you can't help but believe him.

How do you address setbacks or failures with Braeden in the context of their business?

When he was little, I think it was harder. He wanted to make sure he was getting everything right, and we still didn't really know what we were doing and what would be right. I think in many cases, he taught me to let it go. That might be more now since he is older, but when he was little it was more about reflection. When something's happening and you're not sure - like technical difficulties or forgetting something you needed - at that point it's out of your control and it's just realizing that "I'm going to do my best. I can always do better next time." There's never really a failure because even when something doesn't go right, it's a learning experience. I think we both taught each other that not everything's going to be perfect, but at the end of the day, if you're sharing your mission and more people want to hear more from the ripple effect, it won't be a permanent setback. It gave you something to learn from and to improve next time. I feel like it's always been about what's working and not working, then improving it.

Braeden: I think it's good to address it as what you can learn from whatever setback or failure was made and the recovery. "How can I quickly reflect with what I realized was a mistake? And how can I cover it and make it seem not so bad anymore. I think recovery is very important when it comes to failure. Like when I messed up with something public speaking-wise, I was able to bring it back in and just focus.

How do you involve Braeden in the decision-making processes related to his business?

For some parts, he did that on his own - like once he could drive, I wasn't transporting him everywhere. For example, a code purple - which, in Delaware, it means that the temperatures have dropped below freezing and we're opening emergency locations for people to go stay if they don't have a place. I used to do the transporting and he would pack the bags, but he does that now on his own. I would give him the location, sometimes he would take his girlfriend, and they would both go deliver. He has seen me doing things and now he's like "Oh, well I can do that." When it comes to responding to things, he normally will check with me like "Mom, did you see that email? Is it okay?," and I would say, again with my number one question, if he was comfortable with this. When he was younger, it was more like "Do you want me to write an outline for this speech and you fill in the rest? Do you want to practice this?," and then it would get to the point of "No I got it, I can write it. I'll read it through with you." It just naturally happened. I think him seeing me struggle as a single mom, made him always want to fill in.

Teen Biz Parent Guide

Have you noticed any specific interest or talents in your child that align with entrepreneurial pursuits?

Braeden: So, I do like any interactions I can have with the youth and teaching them new things. I've read books to my sister's elementary school and taught many classes of people on food insecurity. I would also say what my mission is and how they can pay it forward in their hometown. I really like that and it goes perfectly with the message I want to spread and helping more people.

Christy: Well, I echo what Braeden said, and I see that he's very good with young people. I think I might have said before that I believe he is even better now at 20 with young people. It's incredible to see how they literally latch on to him. If he walks into a kindergarten room, eight kids are going to be attached immediately. He just has that calming, happy personality. With specific interests, I would say that he is just a natural networker. Even if he's not working for Brae's Brown Bags, he would help other people network. If his friends had an idea, they would go to him. Whether it's a good or bad thing, Braeden is their number one person to go to as a confidant or somebody to get advice. He connects those pieces and almost outlines what they should do and start with. Not just in the nonprofit world, he can naturally connect the dots like a menu for a restaurant or interpersonal issues. For his friends, he is the number one person to go to.

Christy: He did a TED Talk once when he was 12 or 13, and he was the youngest to have done this TEDTalk. He ended up being closer - the last person to do it. You're not supposed to look at anything when you do a TED Talk, and there was a moment where he froze and didn't remember. He had clicked through the slide, but fortunately everyone in the audience were saying "You got this!" You could see him on stage how he breathed, composed himself, and then moved forward. He gave himself the time to do that instead of panicking or crying like I would have, he paused, then moved forward. For me my heart would race, my palms would get sweaty, but not Braeden.

What resources or organizations have been helpful in supporting your child's entrepreneurial journey?

Braeden: Dosomething.org helped us out at the very start. From multiple grants and word of mouth I believe. They helped us with more exposure and the start of my non-profit. After that, we got a lot of support from the YMCA and the Boys & Girls club - where we hold our annual and now biannual celebration of how long 3B has been around. They gave us a place to hold that celebration. The Food Bank has also helped us a lot for the same reason.

Teen Biz Parent Guide

Mainly, we would hold events wherever we could hold them sometimes. When it comes to classes, the only class I took while in middle school would be BPA (Business Professionals of America). It helped my organization - what I was doing at the time and my class went hand in hand with public speaking.

Christy: I work at the Univerwsity of Delaware and I used to work for the College of Agriculture and Natural Resources. They have Delaware Cooperative Extension, which has a while unit that focuses on food insecurity. They were speakers at some events, so having that connection was really great. They also have an annual day event where we could have a table and people could pack brown bags and take them home in the car. So, if you see someone on the street when you're driving, you have a bag and can hand them out the window. The Jefferson Awards were also a big thing year after year. They would help both of us with our leadership skills because they had events where Braeden could work with the young while I worked with the older people. Kohl's, the shopping department, had an award called "Kohl's Cares" which helped too. There was Mazda and NBC Universal as well in doing a lot for helping nonprofits where Braeden received the "Mazda Drive for Good" Award one year. They had him go on "The Today Show" and, at the Christmas tree lighting, he was able to be featured on TV at the Rockefeller Center.

So, having those local connections, working with the Food Bank of Delaware, and the Jefferson Awards, they would then share with us "Look at Kohl's Cares, look at this "Mazda Drive for Good". Dosomething.org was the same - where they help people and kids all over the country to do something good.

How does your child balance the financial aspects of their business, such as budgeting and reinvesting profits?

Christy: Well, as you know, our first donation from Start-a-Snowball that was $100 was gone immediately just because, again, non-perishable healthy foods are so expensive. The brown bags we use aren't plastic bags they're just brown bags, which is something that Mazda helped us with a lot. It's been hard because, as Braeden is getting older, he doesn't qualify anymore for the youth grants. But, we do have a following now - I hate saying "following", since I think we're all leaders - and we have people who regularly donate once a month. So, really, it's basically what the demand is. When we were working with the schools, they had a summer program where kids who didn't have food at home could go get food, and we would help with that. We look for sponsorships when we hold events. That would just be us going to a local mom and pop shop and saying "We're getting ready to do a hunger conference, and we need some money to get this off the floor. Would you like to be a sponsor? Your logo will be on the website and your logo will be on the banner." So, learning how we can amplify local places to make them more visible and to also help us in our initiatives. Working with already existing organizations was also very helpful because they had connections too and we would learn from them like the Food Bank of Delaware.

Humans, in general, want to do good and be told "Your donation 100% goes to this mission." Braeden doesn't get paid, I don't get paid, and we don't do mileage reimbursement - it all comes out of us and our money. When people realize there's no overhead and basically know "we're not using your money for anything, but helping other people," they give, and we're really lucky. When former President Trump was in office, some changes he made like itemized deductions or alike, we hurt from that. We have less donations now that that change is made. So, it's important to know what the policies are and what we can do to incentivize bigger donations like "we'll make sure we tag you on Facebook" or "your logo is gonna be on the email we send out," so things like that. But again, it's never really been about profits, it's just been about being careful with the money and being honest about where it's going.

Braeden: Along with what my mom said, it was a lot of grants and donations that we depended on along with making promises to those who gave us the donations that it would be for good use. If they were a brand or company, they would be included and there's no money-making out of it. Anytime I was on TV, there wouldn't be profits coming to me from that, but I consider the exposure that we got as profitable. We got more good donations and had more people be aware that we are here and helping people.

What advice would you give to a teen or kid entrepreneur who wants to start a business?

Braeden: Something that I always said was to always dream big and that anything you want to do can happen. Not everyone may feel like they have the support they need, especially when they are young, but I'm sure there is at least someone you could talk to about all the things you may or may not want to do. Something to look out for is anyone that you can take your ideas to as long as you know that they will listen and will take your words in account. I think it's always very important to pitch your ideas, or plans for the future, to someone to get other opinions.

Any mistakes that you may think are unforgiving, you can bounce back from almost anything. Always keep at the back of your mind that no matter how hard you fall, you can always get up just as strong as you fell.

Scan this QR code to see Braeden on "The History Channel"

INTERVIEW WITH IRIS PELTON
MOTHER OF APRIL LYNN PELTON

About April Lynn Pelton and Inspired by April

April Lynn Pelton is a motivational speaker, author, and the First Youth Poet Laureate of Tarrant County, that's passionate about sharing her love for reading and writing with others. Since she was two, she has had a passion for reading and developed a love for writing in elementary. During the COVID-19 quarantine, April focused more on her childhood dream of becoming a great author. April has three published books: An Enchanted Tale With A Twist, I AM I CAN I WILL, and The Grove of 100 Wishes. She is currently working on several books, with a soon-to-be-released poetry book that she has worked on with her grandfather, who is also a writer and poet. April has been blessed to have her books in The Dallas Galleria, Stonebriar Mall, The Dock Bookshop, The Arlington Public Library, and featured at several Macy's stores. In addition to working on her business, she believes in giving her best in everything she does. She's an A & B Honor Roll/AP student and Burleson Collegiate HS and is working on her Associate in Liberal Arts at Hill College. April has overcome learning and life challenges with support from her family, friends, and teachers. She believes that having a community of support can help you overcome anything. April's ultimate goal is to create enjoyable reading that allows kids to grow, learn, and develop a love of reading that will last a lifetime.

How a Writing Project Became a Book

During the COVID-19 quarantine, April's parents noticed gaps in her writing while assisting her with assignments. Her mother, a former ELAR teacher and Counselor, asked her 6th Grade English teacher if she could work with her on writing to create her first book. Her teacher agreed, allowing April to focus her attention on working towards a childhood dream. Online learning gave her the opportunity to focus on her writing. She was able to harness her creativity and gift by focusing on specific details, grammar, elaborating her thoughts, and character development. Steps used to assist April in enhancing her craft of writing, were utilized to create a workbook. The ultimate goal for the workbook is to help parents and educators teach basic ELAR concepts and SEL (Social & Emotional Learning) strategies that focus on teaching kindness and building character.

How did your child become interested in entrepreneurship?

My daughter has always loved reading and writing. She has dreamed of becoming an author for as long as I can remember. Her aunt, a business coach, explained to her that she needed a way to market her book because books won't sell themselves, and the best way to make this happen was by creating a business. She started working with her aunt to create logos, a business mission and vision, and branding. I worked with her to create a business post and posts for social media, and her father helped set up an LLC. She also worked on a business pitch for Target Evolution to be part of their youth program. She was selected as one of the vendors at the Dallas location in the Galleria, where she learned more about in-person marketing and pitching. From there, things just took off with her business.

What challenges has your child faced as a young entrepreneur?

She has seen the ups and downs of business, the roadblocks, and the challenges that can sometimes make you want to quit. There have been times when she wanted to quit, and I told her to pray about it before giving up. I'm so glad she has chosen to stick with her dreams and continues using her gift of writing. She also had to make sacrifices, such as hanging out with friends to attend events for her business. Thankfully, our family calendar has helped reduce scheduling conflicts before booking events. Through it all, she has learned a lot about managing and prioritizing things.

How do you, as a parent, support your child in their entrepreneurial endeavors?

We are very supportive and involved parents who believe in helping our children grow. Life is about learning, and we are also learning how to run a business with her. We are researching to find out how to guide her, and she is constantly researching as well. We all work together as a team to build her brand and help her to accomplish her goals. We have to schedule and attend events, help teach her how to manage funds, and market with her. It's a family affair. We are her biggest cheerleaders and fans, as all parents should be, as they root for their kids to win.

Are there specific skills or lessons your child has learned through entrepreneurship?

She has learned business development, branding, public speaking, sacrifice, and determination. She knows what it's like to win and how to accept the times when she doesn't. She has learned how to take a "NO" when marketing but to keep going until she gets a "YES." She has learned the importance of showing up to speak and encourage others, even when she's tired and depleted. She has learned how to balance business with school work, so she's staying on top of her grades. She has learned that she must constantly work on her brand to attract different audiences. She has learned never to give up, even when it gets hard, because someone needs what she has to inspire them to grow.

How do you balance your child's entrepreneurial activities with their academic and social life?

We keep everything on the calendar. Using a family calendar so that everyone knows what's going on has worked for us. As soon as we find out about upcoming opportunities, we check the calendar to ensure they fit into the schedule. She knows to stay on top of her grades because academics are also important in accomplishing her future goals. She plans to attend college, so grades are essential regarding class rank and GPA.

Have you seen any positive changes in your child's confidence or leadership skills since starting their business?

We have watched a shy young lady blossom into a bold, confident young woman. She has shown initiative in participating in activities that have stretched her past her fears and insecurities to grow and achieve significant accomplishments. She is a role model who speaks at many events, and it is impressive to see how she can capture the crowd's attention. This past year, she was named the first Youth Poet Laureate of Tarrant County and is working with a team of professors at Tarrant County College to launch additional workshops for youth for poetry and creative writing. We have seen her become more assertive, utilizing her leadership skills to share ideas and encourage others.

Teen Biz Parent Guide

Do you involve April in decision-making processes related to their business?

Yes, this is essential! When running a business, children must love what they do to grow. They have to attend events, work on marketing plans, have knowledge and expertise on what they are selling, and have a passion for it to continue working at it, especially when things are slow. The reality is that you have to be actively involved for your business to grow. Because it's their vision and dream, they should actively be involved in the decision-making process with guidance. Being actively involved teaches them ownership and responsibility.

How do you address setbacks or failures with April in the context of their business?

April's business has taken many forms and paths. She has always had a goal of publishing a chapter book but has found this challenging. It requires more story development, which she's working on. She has also experienced ups and downs in sales throughout the years. There are times when sales are high and sometimes when sales are low. Through it all, we teach her to focus on using the gifts that God has placed in her. We teach her to focus on always pursuing purpose. When you seek purpose, you won't focus on the challenges that come as much because you know you are doing something bigger than yourself to encourage and inspire others.

Have you noticed any specific interests or talents in your child that align with their entrepreneurial pursuits?

I noticed April's love for writing when she was two. She loved folding and cutting paper to create books. She would draw pictures and tell the family what to write to create her own stories. She also loved going to the library to read. She always said she wanted to be a librarian and an author. She became an author at 12 and has been connected with the Arlington Public Library and Fort Worth Public Library. As a family, we have worked on helping her develop and grow her writing and poetry skills as well as her business and marketing skills.

What resources or organizations have been helpful in supporting your child's entrepreneurial journey?

April's extracurricular activities are writing and business. As parents, we try to find outlets for her to express herself and do what she enjoys. She is a part of several organizations that allow her to do this: Target Evolution, Tarrant County College, and Celebrating You. Through these organizations, she has gained knowledge and exposure to grow her business and develop and enhance her skills.

How does your child balance the financial aspects of their business, such as budgeting and reinvesting profits?

Her goal in creating her business was to share her gift of writing to inspire others and raise money for college. This is why we set up business checking and savings accounts to allow her to grow her business. She knows that 10% goes to tithing, 10% - 20% (depending on her earnings for each event) goes to her, and the remaining goes towards college savings. If she finds something that she would like to invest in to grow her business, we review finances and make decisions from there. We use this as a teaching opportunity to learn fundamental lessons about life, how money works, investing, and business.

ABOUT THE TEMPLATE GUIDE AND TEEN BIZ WORKBOOK

In this section, you will find a treasure trove of practical tools. From customizable business worksheets that will help you guide your child through market research, financial planning, and branding, to ready-to-use templates for crafting compelling elevator pitches and eye-catching business plans, this section helps you work through templates included in the Teen Biz Workbook and equips teens with the essential building blocks for their entrepreneurial journey. Whether they dream of launching the next tech startup or a neighborhood lemonade stand, these resources transform their ideas into actionable steps.

Remember, every successful business started with a spark of imagination and a dash of determination.

- Personal Strengths & Weaknesses
- Lean Startup
- Business Plan vs Pitch Deck
- The Business Model Canvas
- Teen Friendly Business Model Canvas
- Official Business Model Canvas
- Brand Identity Development
- Market Research and Validation
- Startup Budget
- Financial Projection Calculator
- Pitch Deck Template
- One Page Plan and Pitch Notes Worksheet

BUSINESS KNOWLEDGE ASSESSMENT

This assessment will help you and your child determine exactly what you know and may need to learn about business. Rate yourself in each area from 1-5.

Skills	Low		Rating Medium		High
Sales					
Pricing	1	2	3	4	5
Buying	1	2	3	4	5
Sales planning	1	2	3	4	5
Negotiating	1	2	3	4	5
Direct selling to buyers	1	2	3	4	5
Customer service follow up	1	2	3	4	5
Managing other sales reps	1	2	3	4	5
Tracking competitors	1	2	3	4	5
Marketing					
Advertising/promotion/public relations	1	2	3	4	5
Annual marketing plans	1	2	3	4	5
Media planning and buying	1	2	3	4	5
Advertising and copy writing	1	2	3	4	5
Marketing Strategies	1	2	3	4	5
Distribution channel planning	1	2	3	4	5
Pricing	1	2	3	4	5
Packaging	1	2	3	4	5
Financial Planning					
Cash flow planning	1	2	3	4	5
Monthly financial	1	2	3	4	5
Bank relationships	1	2	3	4	5
Management of credit lines	1	2	3	4	5
Accounting					
Bookkeeping	1	2	3	4	5
Billing, payables, receivables	1	2	3	4	5
Monthly profit and loss statements/balance sheets	1	2	3	4	5
Quarterly/annual tax preparation	1	2	3	4	5
Administrative					
Scheduling	1	2	3	4	5
Payroll handling	1	2	3	4	5

Personnel management

Hiring employees	1	2	3	4	5
Firing employees	1	2	3	4	5
Motivating employees	1	2	3	4	5
General management skills	1	2	3	4	5

Personal business skills

Oral presentation skills	1	2	3	4	5
Written communication skills	1	2	3	4	5
Computer skills	1	2	3	4	5
Word processing skills	1	2	3	4	5
Fax, email experience	1	2	3	4	5
Organization skills	1	2	3	4	5

Intangibles

Ability to work long and hard	1	2	3	4	5
Ability to manage risks	1	2	3	4	5
Family support	1	2	3	4	5
Ability to deal with failure	1	2	3	4	5
Ability to work alone	1	2	3	4	5
Ability to work and manage others	1	2	3	4	5

Total

After you've rated yourself in each area, total up the numbers. Then apply the following rating scale:

- ☐ **0-19 points.** If your total is less than 20 points, you should reconsider whether owning a business is the right step for you at this time. If you're sure this is the right step for you, get plenty of coaching and education in the lower rating areas.

- ☐ **20-25 points.** If your total is between 20 and 25 points, you're on the verge of being ready, but you may be wise to spend some time strengthening some of your weaker areas.

- ☐ **26 or more points.** If your total is above 25, you're ready to start a new business now.

_____
_____
_____
_____

LEAN STARTUP METHOD

This workbook will walk you through building a business using the Lean Startup Methodology.

What Is Lean Startup Methodology and How Can You Use It to Build Your Business?

The Lean Startup method, developed by Eric Ries, is a way of starting and running a business that focuses on being efficient, adaptable, and customer-focused. It's like a modern approach to building and growing a company.

In a nutshell, the lean startup is about starting small, learning from customers, and adapting quickly to build a successful business. It's a way of thinking that values flexibility, innovation, and putting the customer at the center of everything you do.

HOW DOES LEAN STARTUP METHODOLOGY HELP ENTREPRENEURS?

The Lean Startup method offers several benefits to entrepreneurs by providing a strategy to build and grow their businesses more effectively. Here's how the lean startup approach can help entrepreneurs, like yourself, in a way that's easy to understand:

Start Smart, Not Big

Instead of jumping into a big, complex project right away, the lean startup suggests you begin with something simple. This helps you test your idea quickly without investing too much time or money upfront.

Learn from People

The lean startup encourages you to talk to the people who might use your product or service. By understanding their needs and preferences, you can create something they'll actually want.

Build and Improve

With the lean startup, you create a small version of your idea and show it to people. Then, you listen to what they say and use their feedback to make it better. It's like making changes to your video game based on what players enjoy most.

Adapt to What Works

If you find out that something isn't quite right with your idea, the lean startup lets you change it without a lot of fuss. You can adjust your game plan and make things better as you go along.

Quick Changes, Less Risk

Imagine you're designing a new level in your video game. With the lean startup, if you don't like how it's turning out, you can change it without wasting too much time. This approach helps you avoid big mistakes and take smaller risks.

Stay Curious and Creative

The lean startup is all about being open to new ideas and trying different things. Just like when you're experimenting with different strategies in a game, you can be creative and find new ways to succeed.

Fail and Learn

Sometimes things won't go as planned, and that's okay! The lean startup teaches you to learn from mistakes quickly, just like when you're figuring out a challenging level in a game. It's all part of the process.

Keep Getting Better

With the lean startup, you don't just create something once and hope for the best. You keep improving and making your idea better based on what you learn from people. It's like leveling up in a game – you're always getting stronger.

So, the lean startup approach is like using your smarts and creativity to build something people love, while being ready to change things up if needed. It's about learning, adapting, and staying curious on your entrepreneurial journey.

What Happened to Writing a Business Plan?

DIFFERENCE BETWEEN BUSINESS PLANS AND LEAN STARTUP

The difference between writing a traditional business plan and adopting the lean startup methodology lies primarily in their approach to business development and planning.

Scope and Detail

Business Plan: Traditional business plans are comprehensive documents that cover various aspects of a business, including market analysis, company description, organizational structure, product or service offerings, marketing strategies, financial projections, and more. They tend to be detailed and often involve extensive research and planning.

Lean Startup: In contrast, the lean startup approach focuses on creating a more concise and dynamic plan. It emphasizes building a minimum viable product (MVP) quickly, testing it in the market, and then iterating based on real-time feedback. The emphasis is on rapid experimentation and learning.

Risk Management

Business Plan: Traditional plans often assume that all the initial assumptions are correct and that the business will unfold according to the outlined strategy. This can pose a higher risk, especially if the market response is different from what was anticipated.

Lean Startup: Lean startup methodology is designed to be more adaptive to uncertainties. It encourages entrepreneurs to identify and test assumptions early on, reducing the risk of investing significant resources in a concept that might not resonate with the market.

Timeline and Iteration

Business Plan: Traditional plans may take a considerable amount of time to develop before any product or service is launched. Changes to the plan may be infrequent and often require a substantial reevaluation of the entire strategy.

Lean Startup: The lean approach values a quicker timeline. Entrepreneurs are encouraged to launch a basic version of their product or service rapidly, gather feedback, and make continuous adjustments. The process involves a series of small iterations, allowing for a more agile response to market dynamics.

Customer-Centric Focus

Business Plan: Traditional plans may focus more on the internal aspects of the business, such as operations and financials, without immediate validation from the target market.

Lean Startup: The lean methodology places a strong emphasis on customer feedback and validation. By engaging with customers early and often, entrepreneurs can refine their offerings based on real-world responses, ensuring a more customer-centric approach.

In summary, while a traditional business plan offers a detailed and structured approach to business development, the lean startup methodology is characterized by its agility, emphasis on experimentation, and continuous adaptation based on customer feedback. The choice between the two often depends on factors such as the nature of the business, market conditions, and the entrepreneur's risk tolerance.

DIFFERENCE BETWEEN BUSINESS PLANS AND A PITCH DECK

Both business plans and pitch decks serve distinct purposes in the realm of entrepreneurship, each playing a crucial role in different stages of a business's development. Here are the key differences between the two:

Purpose and Audience

Business Plan: The business plan is a comprehensive document designed for internal use and potential stakeholders who seek in-depth information about the business. It serves as a roadmap, providing detailed insights into the company's vision, mission, market analysis, financial projections, and operational strategies.

Pitch Deck: A pitch deck, on the other hand, is a concise presentation aimed at external parties, such as investors or potential partners. It serves to capture attention quickly, offering a snapshot of the business idea, its value proposition, and its growth potential.

Format and Length

Business Plan: Business plans are typically longer and more detailed, often spanning multiple pages or sections. They delve into the nuances of various business components, providing a comprehensive overview of the venture.

Pitch Deck: Pitch decks are succinct visual presentations, usually consisting of 10-15 slides. The emphasis is on brevity, focusing on key elements to convey the essence of the business quickly and effectively.

Content Focus

Business Plan: Business plans delve deeply into market research, competition analysis, and operational details. They provide a thorough understanding of the business model, marketing strategy, financial forecasts, and operational intricacies.

Pitch Deck: Pitch decks highlight the most critical aspects of the business, such as the problem being addressed, the solution offered, the target market, the revenue model, and the potential for scalability. The focus is on capturing interest and generating further discussion.

Use in Fundraising

Business Plan: While a business plan is essential for internal planning, it might not be the first document presented to potential investors. Instead, it is often shared after an initial pitch or meeting.

Pitch Deck: Pitch decks are instrumental in the early stages of fundraising. Entrepreneurs use them to attract attention and secure meetings with potential investors. The deck serves as a visual aid during presentations, helping to convey the business concept effectively.

Timeline and Flexibility

Business Plan: Business plans are typically static documents that may be periodically revised. They offer a detailed, long-term perspective on the business.

Pitch Deck: Pitch decks are more dynamic and adaptable. Entrepreneurs often refine and customize them for different audiences or as the business evolves. They are particularly useful in quickly conveying the business idea in dynamic situations.

In essence, while a business plan serves as a comprehensive internal document, a pitch deck is an external-facing tool designed for concise and compelling communication, especially in the context of fundraising and stakeholder engagement.

THE BUSINESS MODEL CANVAS

The Business Model Canvas is a strategic management tool that provides a visual framework for developing, describing, and understanding the key elements of a business model. It was introduced by Alexander Osterwalder and Yves Pigneur in their book "Business Model Generation." The canvas is widely used by entrepreneurs, startups, and established companies to articulate, discuss, and iterate upon their business models in a concise and structured manner.

The Nine Sections of the Business Model Canvas

Customer Segments
Defines the different groups of people or organizations that the business aims to serve. It helps identify the target customers and their specific needs.

Value Propositions
Describes the unique value that the business offers to its customers. It articulates the products or services that address the identified customer needs and differentiates the business from competitors.

Channels
Outlines the various channels through which the business delivers its value propositions to customers. This could include direct sales, online platforms, partnerships, or other distribution methods.

Customer Relationships
Specifies the type of relationship the business establishes with its customers. It could range from personal assistance to self-service, automated services, or community engagement.

Revenue Streams
Identifies the sources of revenue for the business. This block outlines how the business generates income from its customers, whether through sales, subscriptions, licensing, or other revenue models.

Key Resources
Encompasses the critical assets and resources required to deliver the value proposition, reach customers, and operate the business. This may include physical, intellectual, human, or financial resources.

Key Activities
Describes the essential tasks and activities that the business must perform to create and deliver its value proposition, manage relationships, and sustain operations.

Key Partnerships
Identifies external entities, organizations, or suppliers with whom the business collaborates to enhance its capabilities, reduce risk, or access key resources.

Cost Structure
Outlines the major costs and expenses associated with operating the business. This includes both fixed and variable costs, such as production, marketing, and distribution expenses.

The Business Model Canvas is typically presented as a large visual chart, allowing teams to have a comprehensive view of their business model on a single page. It encourages a holistic approach to business strategy and facilitates discussions and iterations as the business evolves. Entrepreneurs find it particularly useful in the early stages of developing and refining their business concepts.

Teen Biz Parent Guide

Teen Friendly Business Model Canvas

The business model canvas is a one-page business plan that helps you think about all of the pieces of your business. Use this template or draw canvas on a large poster board and fill in each box. This canvas will be used later to create your professional business presentation, also known as, a pitch deck.

The most important boxes in the canvas is box 1-5 and box 9. Fill out each box in order from 1-9.

The boxes on the left help you think about all of the costs to operate the business and the boxes on the right help you to think about how the business will make money.

1. My Value
How will my products or services unique to our customers? What will make my business different?

2. Customers
Who will be my customers? Why would they buy from me? What things will all of my customers have in common?

3. Channels
How will my product get to my customers? Am I selling online or in person? Will I ship or deliver?

4. Creating Happy Customers
How will I get customers? How will I keep customers and get them to buy again? How can I grow my customers and encourage them to refer me to others?

5. How We Make Money
How will my business make money? Will we sell directly to customers or businesses? Will we have a subscription or give free trials?

6. Partners and Suppliers
Where do we buy materials and supplies to create our products or run the business? Who provides services to my business to help me operate?

7. Resources
Who will help me operate the business? What do I need to get started? Who do I need to get started?

8. Activities
What do I need to be an expert at doing? What work needs to be done daily, weekly, and monthly? Where will I work?

9. Costs and Expenses
How much money will I need to start the business and keep it going? What do I need to pay for? Who do I need to pay? How much does it cost to create a product to sell?

Official Business Model Canvas with Professional Terms

Key Partners
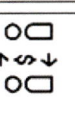
- Partners
- Suppliers
- Resources you use from partners
- Activities performed by partners

Key Activities

- Activities required by your value propositions
- Geographies
- Client relationships
- Revenue streams

Key Resources

- Resources required by your value propositions
- Distribution channels
- Customer relationships
- Revenue streams

Value Propositions
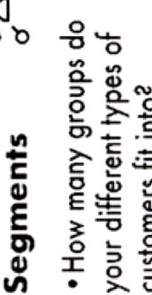
- What value do you deliver to your customer?
- Customer problems you are helping to solve
- Services offered
- Customer needs you are satisfying

Characteristics
- Newness
- Performance
- Customisation
- Getting the job done
- Brand / status
- Price / cost reduction
- Risk reduction
- Accessibility
- Convenience / usability

Customer Relationships
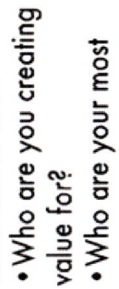
- Expected customer - client relationships
- Which are established?
- How do they fit with the rest of your business model?
- How costly are they?

Channels

- Which channels are your customer using?
- Which do they want to communicate with you on?
- How best to reach them?
- Which are cost effective?

Customer Segments

- How many groups do your different types of customers fit into?
- Who are you creating value for?
- Who are your most important customers?

Cost Structure
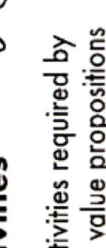
- Key costs in your business model
- Most costly key resources
- Most costly key activities

Revenue Streams
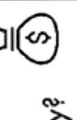
- What do customers most value?
- What are they willing to pay?
- What are they currently paying?
- How are they currently paying?
- How would they like to pay?
- How much does each revenue stream contribute to your overall revenue?

71

Teen Biz Parent Guide

Create your rough draft business model canvas! You will create another one at the end of this section once you have learned more information!

2. Customers		5. How We Make Money
4. Creating Happy Customers	3. Channels	
1. My Value		
7. Resources	8. Activities	9. Costs and Expenses
6. Partners and Suppliers		

72

BENEFITS OF A STRONG BUSINESS BRAND IDENTITY

Having a strong brand identity for a business is like having a superpower that makes the business more awesome. Here are some cool benefits explained in a way that makes sense to teens:

Easy to Recognize
Just like you recognize your friend's voice in a crowd, a strong brand makes the business easy to recognize. When people see the brand's logo, they instantly know it's that company.

Trustworthy and Cool
A strong brand is like a cool character in a game – it makes people trust the business more. When you trust a brand, you're more likely to buy from it.

Stands Out in a Crowd
Imagine you're at a big event, and everyone is wearing the same outfit. A strong brand stands out like a bright costume – it's unique and catches your eye.

Loyal Fans
Just like you're a fan of your favorite game, a strong brand gets loyal fans. People who love the brand keep coming back for more.

Feels Good
A strong brand makes you feel good, just like a fun game. It creates positive feelings and makes people happy to buy from that business.

Same Cool Vibes
Think of your favorite game's style – it's the same in every part of the game. A strong brand has the same cool vibes in everything it does, which makes it reliable.

Confident and Professional
A strong brand is like a confident player – it knows what it's doing and looks professional. This makes people trust the business even more.

Feels Valuable
Just like rare items in a game feel valuable, a strong brand makes the business feel valuable. People are willing to pay more for something they see as special.

Word Spreads Fast
You tell your friends about the awesome games you play, right? A strong brand gets talked about too. When people love it, they tell their friends and the business grows.

Grows Stronger
Like a game with sequels that get better, a strong brand can expand into new things. It helps the business grow and try new ideas.

Lasts a Long Time
Just like games you love never get old, a strong brand can keep the business popular for a long time. It's like the magic that keeps it exciting and successful.

So, a strong brand identity isn't just about a logo – it's about making the business super cool, trustworthy, and loved by everyone who comes across it. It's like giving the business a special boost that helps it stand out and succeed.

TIPS ON NAMING THE BUSINESS

Choosing a name for your business is a crucial decision that can significantly impact your brand identity and market perception. Here are some tips and strategies to help you in the process of naming your business:

Reflect Your Brand
Ensure that the name reflects the essence and values of your business. Consider the products or services you offer, your mission, and the emotions you want your brand to evoke.

Memorability
Aim for a name that is easy to remember. Avoid overly complex or difficult spellings that may confuse potential customers. A memorable name can contribute to word-of-mouth marketing.

Relevance to Industry
Choose a name that conveys what your business is about or the industry you operate in. This helps potential customers quickly understand your offerings.

Avoid Limiting Terms
While relevance is important, avoid using terms that may limit your business's growth or expansion. Ensure the name can accommodate potential diversification or changes in your product or service offerings.

Check Availability
Before finalizing a name, check the availability of the corresponding domain name for your website and ensure that the name is not already in use by another business in your industry. This is crucial for online visibility.

Trademark Search
Conduct a thorough trademark search to ensure that the name is not already registered or in use by another business. This helps prevent legal issues and protects your brand.

Consider Future Marketing and Branding
Envision how the name will look on your logo, business cards, and marketing materials. Ensure it is visually appealing and can be easily incorporated into your overall branding strategy.

Simplicity and Pronunciation
Choose a name that is easy to pronounce and spell. This facilitates communication and reduces the likelihood of misunderstandings.

Test with Your Target Audience
Get feedback from your target audience. Conduct surveys or informal interviews to gauge their reactions to potential names. This can provide valuable insights and help you choose a name that resonates with your audience.

Check Cultural Connotations
Be mindful of cultural connotations associated with words or phrases in different languages. You want to avoid unintentional meanings that may have negative implications.

Create a Unique Identity
Aim for a name that sets your business apart from competitors. A unique and distinctive name can contribute to a strong brand identity.

Think Long-Term
Consider the long-term implications of the name. Will it still be relevant and effective as your business grows? Avoid trendy names that may quickly become outdated.

Remember, the name you choose is a critical element of your brand, and investing time and thought into the process can pay off in building a strong and memorable brand identity.

BRAND COLOR PSYCHOLOGY AND MEANINGS

Color psychology is a fascinating field that explores how colors impact human behavior and emotions. When it comes to marketing and branding, leveraging the right colors can significantly influence purchasing decisions. Here are some intriguing insights:

1. First Impressions: Up to 90% of a consumer's initial impression is influenced by color. When someone encounters your brand or product, the hues they perceive play a crucial role in shaping their perception.
2. Brand Awareness: Color can increase brand awareness and recognition by a whopping 80%. Think about iconic logos like Facebook's blue or Coca-Cola's red—they stick in our minds because of their consistent use of color.
3. Visual Impact: A staggering 93% of consumers make purchasing decisions based on visuals alone. The colors you choose can evoke specific emotions and associations, affecting how people perceive your brand.

WHY COLORS MATTER TO YOUR BUSINESS

RED	Passion	Aggression	Intense
ORANGE	Energy	Fun	Warmth
YELLOW	Happiness	Optimism	Youth
GREEN	Healing	Success	Hope
BLUE	Loyalty	Stability	Tranquility
PURPLE	Royalty	Spirituality	Luxury
BROWN	Stability	Natural	Reliability
BLACK	Power	Mystery	Professional
GRAY	Neutral	Practical	Quiet
WHITE	Purity	Cleanliness	Innocence

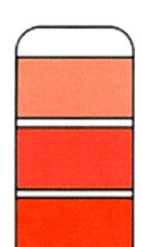

RED: THE MOST STIMULATING COLOR
- PROMPTS ACTION
- SYMBOLIZES PASSION
- CAN BE OVERSTIMULATING

COMMON ASSOCIATIONS: POWER, ENERGY, IMPORTANCE, AGGRESSION, DRAMA, INTENSITY

PURPLE: POPULAR AMONG WOMEN
- HISTORIC TIES TO ROYALTY
- SYMBOLIZES LUXURY
- GENERALLY DISLIKED BY MEN

COMMON ASSOCIATIONS: ELEGANCE, MYSTERY, IMAGINATION, WISDOM, SPIRITUALITY, SENSUALITY, CREATIVITY

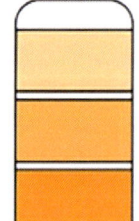

ORANGE: A "FRIENDLIER" RED
- CREATES A SENSE OF HASTE
- SYMBOLIZES MOVEMENT
- CAN BE POLARIZING

COMMON ASSOCIATIONS: ENERGY, FRIENDLINESS, INDIVIDUALITY, PHYSICAL ACTIVITY, CONFIDENCE

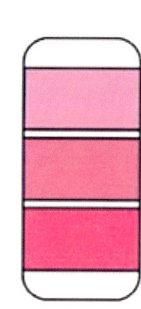

PINK: THE MISUNDERSTOOD COLOR
- BEST USED WITH BABY PRODUCTS
- STIMULATES THE SWEET TOOTH
- FALSELY BELIEVED AS A FAVORITE AMONG WOMEN

COMMON ASSOCIATIONS: CANDY, TREATS, BABIES

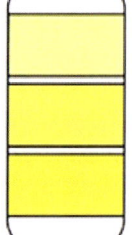

YELLOW: COMFORT AND INVIGORATION
- HEIGHTENS EMOTIONS
- PROMOTES ENTHUSIASM
- CAN CAUSE ANXIETY

COMMON ASSOCIATIONS: PLAYFULNESS, HAPPINESS, FUN

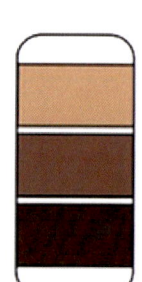

BEIGE: THE "WILDCARD OF COLORS"
- FAVORED OVER BROWN
- PROMOTES COLORS AROUND IT
- CAN BE TOO DULL ON ITS OWN

COMMON ASSOCIATIONS: OUTDOORS, RUGGEDNESS, HUMILITY, DEPENDABILITY, EARTHINESS

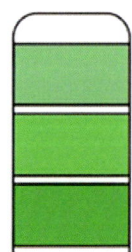

GREEN: CONNECTS WARM AND COOL
- IMPLIES BALANCE AND STABILITY
- ASSOCIATED WITH NATURE
- FRESH ENERGY AND GROWTH

COMMON ASSOCIATIONS: CREATIVITY, WELL-BEING, INNOVATION, MONEY, AFFLUENCE, ENVIRONMENT, SUCCESS

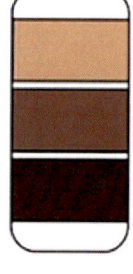

WHITE: A QUIET POWERHOUSE
- BEST FOR ACCENTING COLORS
- PROMOTES A SENSE OF CALM
- CAN BE REPLACED WITH IVORY

COMMON ASSOCIATIONS: PURITY, CALMNESS, SIMPLICITY, VIRTUE, STERILITY, ALOOFNESS

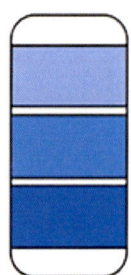

BLUE: THE MOST TRUSTWORTHY
- PROMOTES RELAXATION
- EXTREMELY VERSATILE COLOR
- NOT IDEAL FOR FOOD WEBSITES

COMMON ASSOCIATIONS: INTELLIGENCE, SERENITY, RELIABILITY, REFRESHING IDEAS, SINCERITY

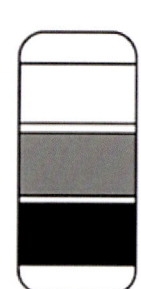

BLACK: THE SOPHISTICATED COLOR
- ADAPTS TO ITS ACCENT COLORS
- TIMELESS AND CLASSIC
- CAN BE TOO DOMINATING

COMMON ASSOCIATIONS: LUXURY, VALUE, ELEGANCE, POWER, EDGINESS, FORMALITY, EXCLUSIVITY

MONOGRAM LOGOS   LETTERFORM LOGO   WORDMARK LOGO

PICTORIAL MARKS   MASCOTS LOGOS   ABSTRACT LOGO

EMBLEM LOGO   COMBINATION MARK   SLIME LOGO

DYNAMIC LOGO

© webneel.com

MARKET RESEARCH AND MARKET VALIDATION

Market Research

There are two kinds of market research: primary and secondary.

Primary research means gathering your own data. For example, you could do a traffic count at a proposed location, use the Yellow Pages to identify competitors, and do surveys or focus-group interviews to learn about consumer preferences. Professional market research can be very costly, but many books show small business owners how to do effective research themselves.

Secondary research means using published information such as industry profiles, trade journals, newspapers, magazines, census data, and demographic profiles. This type of information is available in public libraries, industry associations, chambers of commerce, from vendors who sell to your industry, and from government agencies.

There are more online sources than you could use. Your chamber of commerce has good information on your local area. Trade associations and trade publications often have excellent industry-specific data. To create a marketing strategy, be as specific as possible. Give statistics, numbers, and sources.

Market Validation

Market validation in the context of the Lean Startup methodology refers to the process of testing and validating key assumptions about a business idea or product within the target market. The goal is to gather real-world feedback from potential customers to determine whether there is a genuine demand for the proposed product or service before investing significant time and resources. Market validation is a crucial step in the lean startup approach as it helps entrepreneurs mitigate risks and make informed decisions based on validated insights.

Here are key aspects of market validation within the Lean Startup framework:

Hypothesis Testing
Entrepreneurs begin by forming hypotheses about their business model, including assumptions about the target customers, their needs, and the value proposition. These hypotheses are the foundation for subsequent validation efforts.

Minimum Viable Product (MVP)
Instead of developing a fully-fledged product, the lean startup methodology advocates for creating a Minimum Viable Product (MVP). An MVP is a simplified version of the product that contains essential features to test the core value proposition.

Build-Measure-Learn Cycle
Entrepreneurs follow a continuous feedback loop known as the Build-Measure-Learn cycle. They build the MVP, measure its performance and impact in the market, and then learn from the gathered data to make informed adjustments and improvements.

Customer Feedback
Actively seek feedback from potential customers. This can involve surveys, interviews, or observing user behavior with the MVP. The goal is to understand whether the product addresses a real pain point and if customers find value in the solution.

Pivot or Persevere
Based on the feedback received, entrepreneurs decide whether to pivot (make significant changes to the product or business model) or persevere (continue with the current approach). The lean startup methodology encourages adaptability and flexibility in response to market dynamics.

Validation Metrics
Establish key metrics to measure the success or failure of the MVP. These metrics should align with the business objectives and provide quantifiable data to evaluate the viability of the product.

Iterative Process
Market validation is an iterative process. Entrepreneurs make incremental adjustments to the product and its positioning based on continuous feedback and learning. This iterative approach allows for a more responsive and adaptive development process.

Rapid Experimentation
Conduct rapid and low-cost experiments to test critical assumptions. By using quick and efficient methods, entrepreneurs can validate or invalidate hypotheses without committing extensive resources upfront.

Risk Reduction
The primary aim of market validation is to reduce the risk of investing in a product or business model that may not resonate with the market. By validating assumptions early and often, entrepreneurs can make more informed decisions and allocate resources effectively.

Market validation in the Lean Startup methodology is about learning quickly and adjusting course based on real-world evidence. It is a proactive approach to building a sustainable and customer-focused business by ensuring that the product or service meets a genuine market need.

HOW CUSTOMER SURVEYS HELP BUILD PRODUCTS AND BUSINESSES

Customer surveys play a crucial role in building products and businesses by providing valuable insights into customer preferences, needs, and opinions. Here are several ways in which customer surveys contribute to the development and growth of products and businesses:

Understanding Customer Needs

Surveys help businesses gain a deeper understanding of their customers' needs and preferences. By directly asking customers about their challenges, preferences, and desires, businesses can tailor their products to better meet customer expectations.

Product Improvement

Feedback gathered through surveys can highlight areas of improvement for existing products. Understanding what customers like or dislike about a product allows businesses to make informed decisions about refining features, enhancing quality, or addressing specific pain points.

Identifying Market Gaps

Surveys enable businesses to identify potential market gaps or unmet needs. By asking questions about current solutions and competitors, businesses can discover areas where there may be opportunities to differentiate and offer something new or better.

Validating Ideas

Before investing significant resources in product development, businesses can use surveys to validate their ideas. By presenting concepts or prototypes to potential customers and gauging their reactions, businesses can assess the viability and market acceptance of a new product.

Customer Segmentation

Surveys help in segmenting the customer base. By understanding the diverse needs and preferences of different customer segments, businesses can tailor their marketing strategies and product offerings to specific target groups.

Determining Pricing Strategies

Surveys can provide insights into customers' willingness to pay for certain features or products. This information is valuable in determining pricing strategies that align with perceived value and affordability for the target market.

Gathering Competitive Intelligence

Businesses can use surveys to gather information about competitors and market trends. Questions about competitors' products, strengths, and weaknesses can inform strategic decision-making and help businesses position themselves effectively in the market.

Building Customer Loyalty

Demonstrating that a business values customer opinions through surveys can enhance customer loyalty. It shows a commitment to continuous improvement and a willingness to listen, fostering a positive relationship between the business and its customer base.

Launching Effective Marketing Campaigns

Surveys can provide insights into the most effective marketing channels and messages. Understanding where customers gather information and how they make purchasing decisions helps businesses tailor their marketing campaigns for maximum impact.

Risk Mitigation

By seeking customer feedback early in the product development process, businesses can identify and address potential issues before a product is launched. This proactive approach reduces the risk of product failure and negative customer reactions.

Iterative Development

Continuous customer feedback through surveys supports an iterative development process. Businesses can make incremental improvements based on ongoing insights, ensuring that products evolve in response to changing customer needs and market dynamics.

In summary, customer surveys serve as a powerful tool for businesses to gather actionable insights, validate ideas, and make informed decisions throughout the product development lifecycle. By engaging with customers through surveys, businesses can build products that resonate with their target audience, ultimately contributing to long-term success and growth.

SURVEY QUESTIONS

Feel free to adjust the questions to align with your specific business or idea.

1. What are your favorite household items or products to buy? (For example, t-shirts, cups, mugs, backpacks or bags, etc..)
2. Why do you prefer purchasing these items?
3. How much do you typically spend on these items?
4. What colors do you prefer when buying these items?
5. How often do you purchase these items? a. Daily b. Weekly c. Monthly d. Quarterly e. Yearly
6. Did you find this survey helpful? How can we improve our surveys in the future to better serve your needs?
7. What other product or service ideas do you suggest for a teen small business owner?

CREATING A STARTUP BUDGET

You will have many expenses before you even begin operating your business. It's important to estimate these expenses accurately and then to plan where you will get sufficient funding.

Even with the best of research, however, opening a new business has a way of costing more than you think. There are two ways to make allowances for surprise expenses. The first is to add a little "padding" to each item in the budget. The problem with that approach, however, is that it destroys the accuracy of your plan. The second approach is to add a separate line item, called "contingencies" or "miscellaneous", to account for the unforeseeable. This is the approach we recommend.

Talk to others who have started similar businesses to get a good idea of how much to allow for contingencies. If you cannot get good information, we recommend a rule of thumb that contingencies should equal at least 20 percent of the total of all other start-up expenses.

BUSINESS BUDGET TEMPLATE

Monthly Gross Revenue

Price of Product	
Cost to Make Product (How much did it cost to make 1 product?)	
Monthly Sales Volume (How many will you sell in 1 week? Multiply the number times 4.)	
Gross Revenue (Multiply the price of product times the Monthly Sales Volume)	
Cost of Goods Sold (Multiply the Cost to Make Product times the Sales Volume)	
Gross Profit (Subtract Cost of Goods Sold from Gross Revenue)	
Monthly Gross Profit	

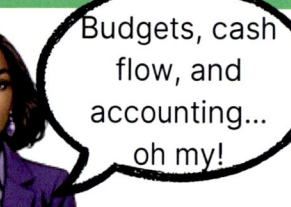

"Budgets, cash flow, and accounting… oh my!"

Monthly Fixed Expenses Now subtract your expenses	
Website	
Marketing and Advertising	
Phone	
Transportation	
Contingencies	
Other Expenses: _____	
Other Expenses: _____	
Total Monthly Fixed Expenses (add up everything in this section and put the total here)	
Net Profit	
Net Profit (Subtract Monthly Fixed Expenses in the section above from the Monthly Gross Profit in the top section)	
If it's a positive number, you made a profit! If it's negative, you're losing money	

Here are some tips to make sure you're making money!

1. Sell more products or increase your sales volume per week. Instead of selling 5 products, try to sell 10 or 15 and recalculate your budget.

2. Reduce the cost of making a product. Sometimes you can order items in bulk to reduce costs or find cheaper supplies and materials. Try to reduce your cost to make a product by $1 and recalculate your budget.

3. Reduce expenses. Find ways to reduce your monthly expenses. See if you can use a free website or choose a website that is $5-$10 a month instead of $20 a month. Find ways to market and advertise free instead of spending money, such as encouraging your followers and customers to refer others to your business.

Financial Projection Calculator

Think you're a budget pro? Well let's add some components to the budget! Use this online calculator to calculate your profits (or losses) from 1 month – 12 months. Visit teenbizbox.com to download and use this worksheet. Adjust your numbers until it makes sense!

Financial Template

How to Use this Template:
<- Only enter data into the "Green" cells. The white cells are formula driven and will calculate automatically.
- yellow boxes is how you increase your net profit
- personal expenses (budget your personal expenses with this number)

Weekly Gross Revenue		
Price (Gross Revenue)	$	-
Cost of Goods Sold	$	-
Gross Profit Margin	$	-
Weekly Sales Volume		
Weekly Gross Profit	$	-

Packaging Cost and Inventory
Sales/Day = 0

Monthly Fixed Expenses:		
Website	$	-
Rent (Pop Up/Vendor Booths)	$	-
Phone	$	-
Transportation	$	-
Quickbooks Acct.	$	-
Marketing / Advertising	$	-
Monthly Total	$	-

Expenses Per/Wk = $0.00

Weekly Labor Expenses		
Hours Worked		0
My Wages/Hour	$	-
Labor Expense	$	-

Monthly Wages
My Money/Week $0.00

Gross Profit		
Weekly	$	-
Monthly	$	-
Annual	$	-

Fixed Expenses + Labor		
Weekly	$	-
Monthly	$	-
Annual	$	-

Net Profit		
Weekly	$	-
Monthly	$	-
Annual	$	-

	Breakeven Sales Volume/Weekly
	#DIV/0!
	Breakeven Sales Volume/Monthly
	#DIV/0!
	Breakeven Sales Volume/Annually
	#DIV/0!

Financial Projections Slide

	1 Month	6 Months	12 Months
Gross Revenue	$0	$0	$0
Cost of Sales	$0	$0	$0
Gross Profit Margin			
Expenses	$0	$0	$0
Net Profit	$0	$0	$0

*You can adjust your sales volume and other expenses to include growing your sales during the year. For example, if you're "Weekly Sales Volume" is 40 units per week for Month 1, then maybe by Month 6 you're selling 100 units per week. You can adjust this template to reflect the increased volume you desire and use those numbers on your financial slide

What to do with left over Net Profit? Follow Below:

Save	20%
Reinvest	45%
Cash Cushion	25%
Repay Investors/Loans	10%
Total Percentage	100%

PITCH DECK TEMPLATE

Use this template to create a professional presentation for your business that you can use to win pitch competitions or share with others about what your company does. Use lots of pictures and images and keep text to a minimum. This is best used when presenting to investors or raising funds for your business. Write notes on what you'll include on each slide on the lines below the slide.

Business Name and Logo Slide

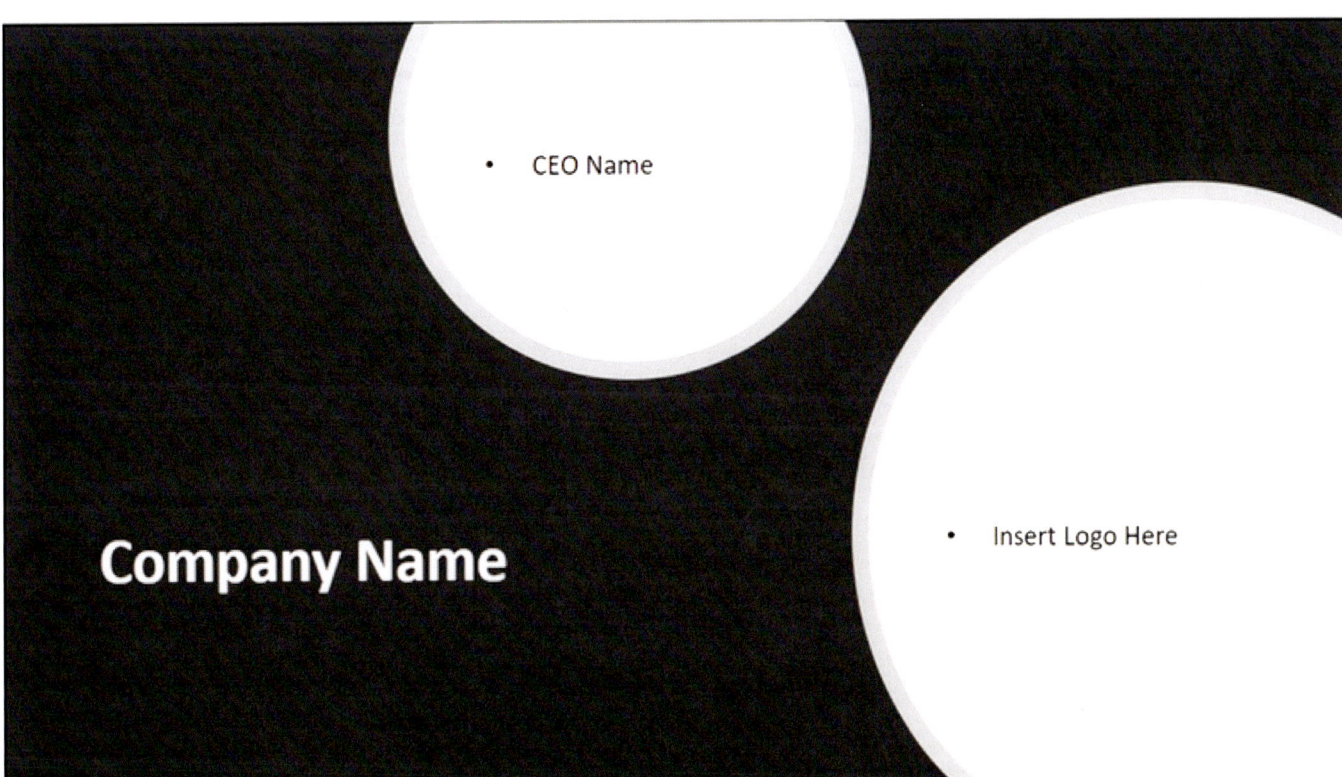

The Problem Slide includes facts and statistics to communicate the problem you are solving and why it is a problem.

Teen Biz Parent Guide

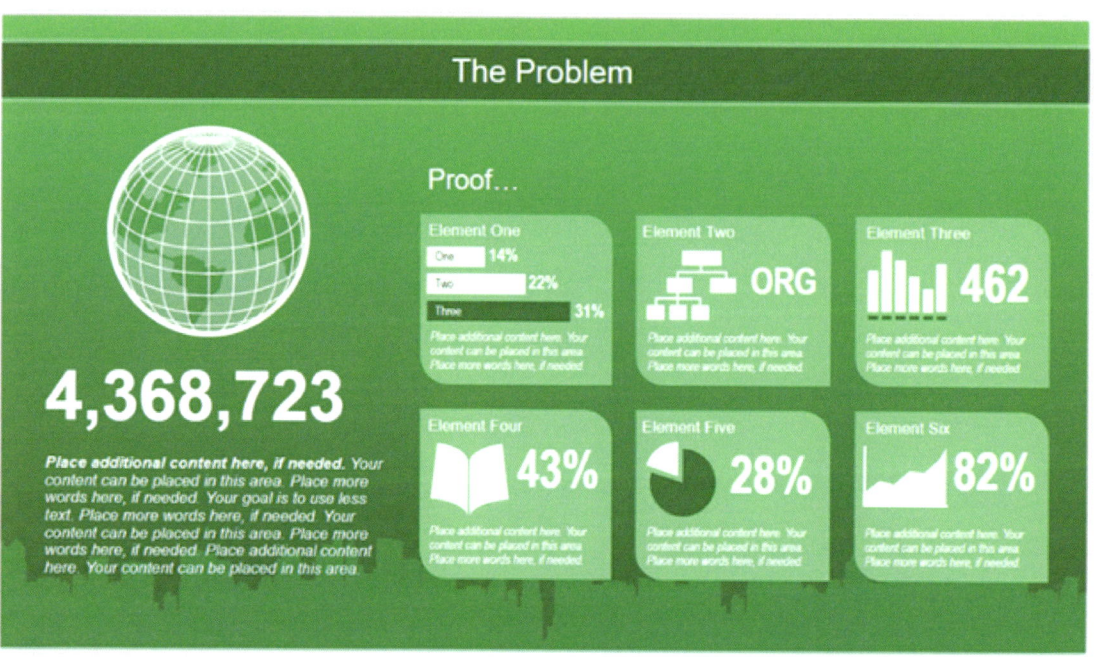

The Solution Slide includes information about your business and how it solves the problem and why it works.

Products and Services Slide is brief overview of the features and benefits of your products or services

Customer Profile and Target Audience Slide shares information about your ideal customers and how many customers need your product in your local community, state, or nationally.

Teen Biz Parent Guide

Customer/Target Audience Demographics

Who is our Target Audience?

- Males
- Ages 18-29
- Like video games
- Located in Houston and Katy
- Recent High school or college grads

5 Facts about our Target Audience or Market

The population of our target audience locally, statewide, and nationally

- $159 billion dollar industry
- $16.5 million males play video games ages 18-29 (or 72% of male Americans)
- Austin ranked sixth with a score of 60.02 and is the only Texas city to rank in the top 10. Other Texas cities in the top 50 include San Antonio (24), Houston (30), Plano (40), Garland (44), and Dallas (49)

Competitive Analysis

Who are our competitors?

- Electronic Arts
- Hasboro
- Candy Crush Saga

	Competitor 1	My Company
Pricing		
		Competitor 2

Quality

My Company	Competitor 1	Competitor 2
Lowest Price	Most expensive	Average Price
Best Quality	Low Quality	Good Quality

Competitive Analysis Slide provides information about how you compare to your competitors

Goals and Milestones Slide shows what you have accomplished so far and what your goals are for the next one to five years.

Financial Projections Slide provides a short overview of the annual revenue, expenses, and net profit of the business

Teen Biz Parent Guide

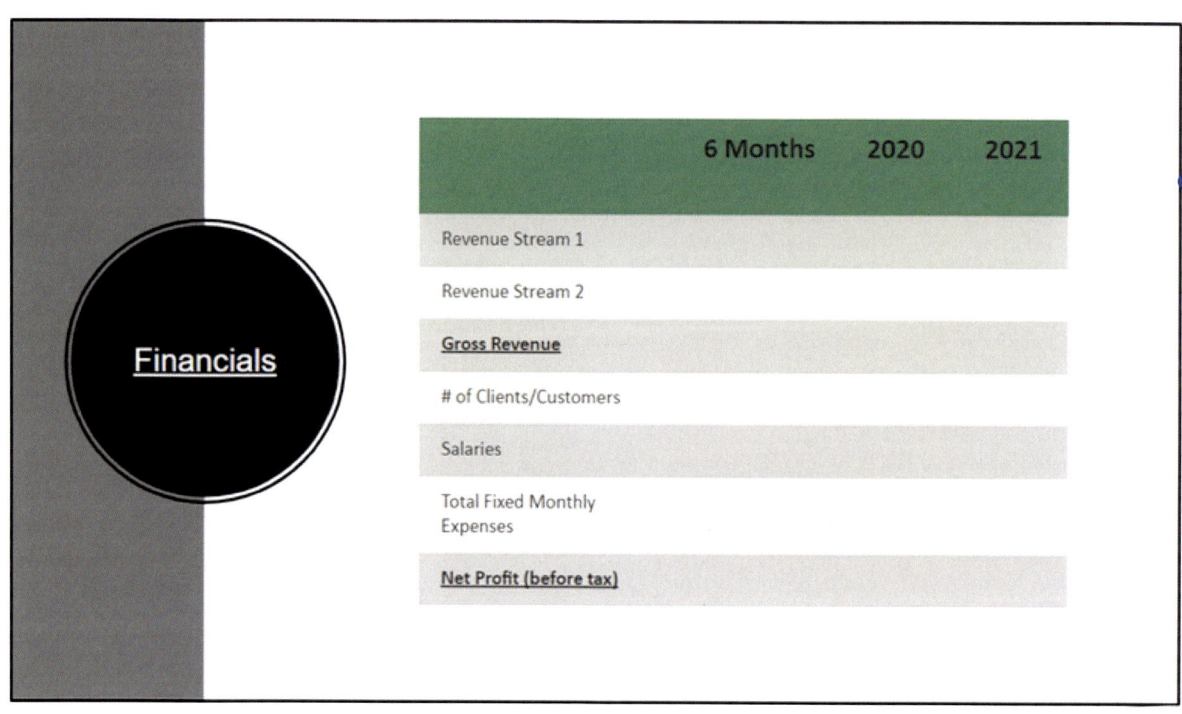

Notes about financials and calculations:

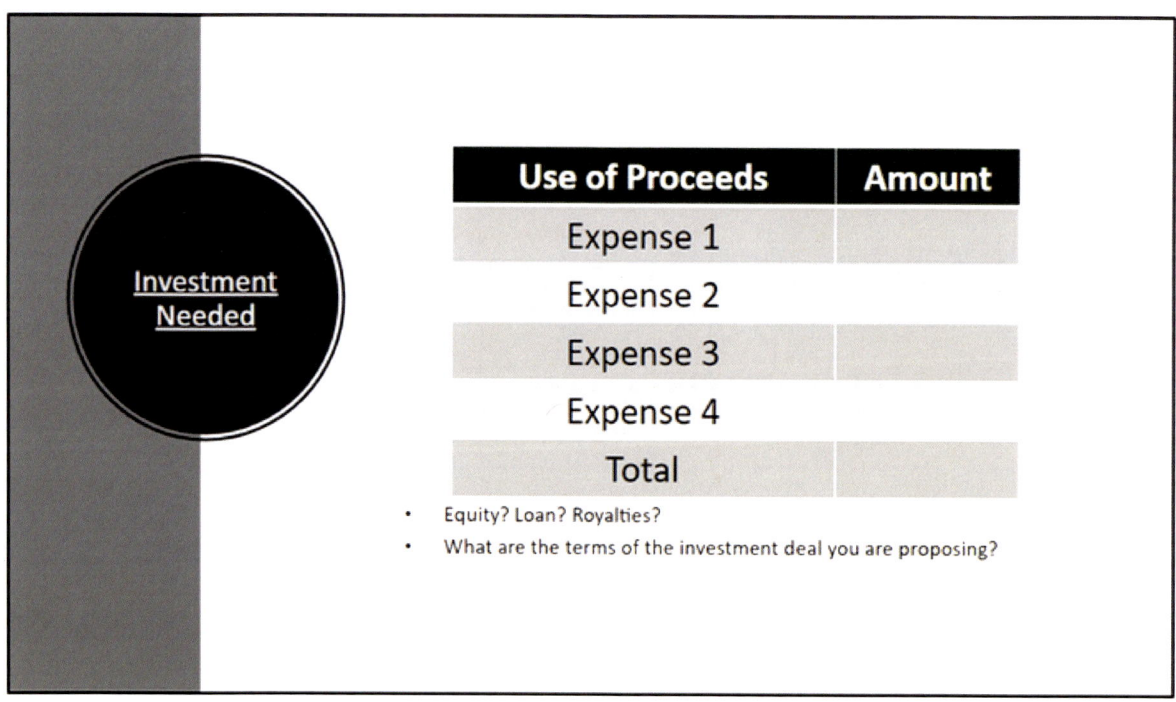

Use of Proceeds Slide explains how you intend to use the funds from an investment or loan to grow your business.

The Closing Slide is a summary of the key points of your business or idea and provides information to contact you.

Teen Biz Parent Guide

ONE PAGE BUSINESS PLAN AND PITCH NOTES WORKSHEET

Use this worksheet to summarize the important parts of your business or idea that you have detailed using your business model canvas, pitch deck, and this workbook.

1 – 2 SENTENCE MAX PER RESPONSE

WHAT + HOW + WHO	WHAT do we do?	
	HOW do we do it?	
	WHO do we serve?	
WHY	DEFINE CUSTOMER PROBLEM	
	DEFINE SOLUTION PROVIDED	
REVENUE	PRICING + BILLING STRATEGIES	
	INCOME STREAMS	
MARKETING	CUSTOMER REACH STRATEGY	
	REFERRAL GENERATION STRATEGY	
COMPETITION	TOP COMPETITORS	
	OUR COMPETITIVE ADVANTAGE	
METRICS	SUCCESS MILESTONE MARKER 1	
	SUCCESS MILESTONE MARKER 2	

SITUATIONAL ANALYSIS (SWOT)

INTERNAL FACTORS	
STRENGTHS (+)	WEAKNESSES (–)

EXTERNAL FACTORS	
OPPORTUNITIES (+)	THREATS (–)

Teen Biz Parent Guide

TIPS FOR PARENTS

Supporting a young entrepreneur as a parent can be both exciting and challenging. Here are some tips to help you guide and nurture your kid entrepreneur:

- **Encourage Their Interests:** Pay attention to your child's interests and passions. Encourage them to explore these areas as potential business ideas. When they're passionate about what they're doing, they're more likely to stay motivated and committed.
- **Teach Business Basics:** Introduce them to fundamental business concepts like budgeting, pricing, marketing, and customer service. This early exposure can help them develop a strong foundation for their entrepreneurial journey.
- **Provide Guidance, Not Control:** While it's important to offer guidance, avoid being overly controlling. Let them make decisions, take calculated risks, and learn from their mistakes. This independence will foster their problem-solving skills and resilience.
- **Set Realistic Expectations:** Help your child set realistic goals for their business. While it's great to dream big, make sure their expectations align with their resources, time, and abilities. This can prevent frustration and disappointment.
- **Focus on Learning:** Emphasize that learning and growth are the primary goals, rather than immediate financial success. This mindset shift can reduce pressure and allow your child to focus on building skills and gaining experience.
- **Time Management:** Balancing school, social life, and a business can be challenging for young entrepreneurs. Teach them effective time management skills to ensure they don't become overwhelmed.
- **Networking and Mentoring:** Encourage your child to connect with other young entrepreneurs, mentors, and professionals in their field. Networking can provide valuable insights, guidance, and potential collaboration opportunities.
- **Financial Literacy:** Teach them the basics of money management, including saving, investing, and budgeting. Help them understand the financial aspects of running a business and making informed decisions.
- **Celebrate Milestones:** Recognize and celebrate their achievements, whether they're big or small. This positive reinforcement can boost their confidence and motivation.
- **Failure is a Learning Opportunity:** Teach your child that failure is a natural part of entrepreneurship. When things don't go as planned, help them analyze what went wrong and how they can improve in the future.
- **Ethics and Values:** Instill a strong sense of ethics and values in your child's business practices. Teach them the importance of honesty, integrity, and treating customers and partners with respect.
- **Physical and Mental Well-being:** Entrepreneurship can be demanding, so ensure your child takes care of their physical and mental health. Encourage a balanced lifestyle that includes exercise, proper nutrition, and relaxation.
- **Legal and Safety Considerations:** Depending on the nature of the business, teach them about legal requirements, safety regulations, and any necessary permits or licenses.
- **Patience and Perseverance:** Entrepreneurship requires patience and perseverance. Help your child understand that success takes time and that setbacks are temporary roadblocks, not dead ends.
- **Stay Involved:** While giving them independence, stay involved in their entrepreneurial journey by showing genuine interest, asking questions, and offering your support.

Remember, the key is to create a supportive and nurturing environment where your young entrepreneur feels empowered to learn, grow, and pursue their passions.

TEACHING KIDS HOW TO BUILD CREDIT AND MANAGE IT

Teaching kids about credit and helping them build their credit history can be a valuable educational experience. However, it's important to approach this process carefully and responsibly. Here's a step-by-step guide on how to train kids to build credit:

Understanding the Basics

Begin by explaining fundamental credit concepts in simple terms. Discuss what credit is, why it's important, and how it works using relatable examples.

Teach Financial Literacy

Before delving into credit, ensure your kids have a solid understanding of financial literacy. Cover topics like budgeting, saving, distinguishing needs from wants, and cultivating responsible spending habits.

Authorized User on a Parent's Account

If your child is a teenager, consider adding them as an authorized user on one of your credit card accounts. This allows them to benefit from your positive credit history, but make sure they understand the responsibilities and limits involved.

Secured Credit Card

When your child reaches eligibility (usually at 18), assist them in opening a secured credit card. With a secured card, they provide a cash deposit as collateral, which also determines their credit limit. This method provides a safe way to initiate independent credit building.

Monitor and Educate

Stress the importance of regularly monitoring credit activity. Help your child review credit card statements, track spending, and comprehend how credit utilization impacts their credit score.

Responsible Credit Usage

Educate your child on responsible credit card usage, emphasizing the necessity of paying their credit card bill in full and on time every month to avoid accruing interest charges.

Managing Credit Utilization

Explain credit utilization—the ratio of credit used to the total credit limit. Encourage your child to maintain a credit utilization ratio below 30% to uphold a healthy credit score.

Building a Credit History

Encourage your child to use their credit card for small, routine purchases and promptly pay off the balance each month. This demonstrates responsible credit management and contributes to establishing a positive credit history.

Credit Education Resources

Provide educational materials such as articles, videos, and books focusing on credit building and personal finance to deepen your child's understanding of credit-related concepts.

Credit Building Apps

Research and consider utilizing apps designed to assist users in building credit, such as those reporting rent payments or offering credit-builder loans, to aid your child in their credit-building journey.

Setting Goals

Help your child establish financial goals related to credit. For instance, they could aim to achieve a specific credit score within a set timeframe or save up for a significant purchase they may eventually finance through credit.

Long-Term Financial Planning

Teach your child that building credit is a gradual process with long-term benefits. Discuss how maintaining good credit can lead to favorable interest rates on loans and credit cards, better rental terms, and even enhanced job opportunities.

Remember, building credit requires patience and diligence. It's crucial to instill in your child the importance of responsible credit management to steer clear of debt pitfalls. By offering guidance, teaching financial principles, and enabling them to practice responsible credit use, you're equipping them with essential skills for managing their finances effectively throughout their lives.

TEACHING KIDS ABOUT THE STOCK MARKET

The stock market is like a place where people can buy and sell ownership shares of companies. It's a way for companies to raise money and for individuals to invest in those companies. Here's a simple explanation:

Ownership Shares

Imagine a company as a big pizza. When a company wants to raise money to grow or invest, it divides the pizza into smaller slices called "shares." These shares represent ownership in the company.

Publicly Traded Companies

Some companies decide to sell their shares to the public. This means anyone, including regular people like you, can buy a piece of the company. These companies are called "publicly traded companies."

Stock Exchanges

The stock market is where shares of these publicly traded companies are bought and sold. It's like a big marketplace where people trade ownership in companies. Major stock exchanges include the New York Stock Exchange (NYSE) and the Nasdaq.

Buying and Selling

When you buy shares of a company, you become a shareholder. This means you own a small part of the company. When you sell your shares, you're giving up your ownership.

Investing and Profits

People buy shares of companies as investments. They hope that as the company grows and does well, the value of their shares will increase. This can lead to profits if they decide to sell their shares at a higher price than they paid.

Risks and Rewards

Investing in the stock market can be rewarding, but it also involves risks. If a company doesn't do well, the value of its shares can go down, and investors might lose money.

Diversification

To manage risks, investors often diversify, which means spreading their money across different companies and industries. This way, if one company's shares go down, the impact on their overall investment is minimized.

Long-Term Perspective

Investing in the stock market is generally more effective over the long term. It's not about quick gains, but rather letting your investment grow over many years.

Market Fluctuations

The value of shares can go up and down due to various factors like company performance, economic conditions, and global events. This is why the stock market can be unpredictable.

Learning and Research

If you're interested in investing in the stock market, it's important to do your research and learn about the companies you're considering investing in.

Remember, the stock market is a way for companies to grow and for people to potentially grow their money, but it's important to be informed and make investment decisions that align with your financial goals and risk tolerance.

HOW TO GET STARTED LEARNING HOW TO TRADE STOCKS

Getting started with learning how to trade stocks involves a combination of education, research, and practical experience. Learning about the stock market can be both educational and potentially beneficial in the long run. Here's a step-by-step guide to get you started:

Understand the Basics
Begin by learning the fundamental concepts of the stock market. Research terms like stocks, shares, dividends, stock exchanges, and how buying and selling works.

Read Books and Online Resources
Explore beginner-friendly books and online articles that explain the stock market in simple terms. Look for resources written for teens or beginners.

Watch Educational Videos
Utilize platforms like YouTube, which offer plenty of videos breaking down stock market concepts visually. Look for channels that offer explanations and tutorials for beginners.

Follow Financial News
Stay updated on stock market trends, companies, and economic developments by following financial news websites, apps, or TV channels.

Explore Virtual Simulators
Practice buying and selling stocks with virtual money using virtual stock market simulators. This helps you understand how things work without risking real money.

Online Courses
Look for online courses or webinars specifically designed for beginners in the stock market. Some are free, and others might have a small fee.

Learn from Experts
Follow credible financial experts and investors on social media platforms like Twitter or LinkedIn. They often share valuable insights and advice.

Paper Trading
Simulate stock trading without real money. Keep a record of the trades you have made and see how your decisions turn out.

Understand Risk and Reward
Learn about the concept of risk and reward in investing. Understand that higher potential returns often come with higher risks.

Read Company Reports
Start reading annual reports and financial statements of companies to gain insights into their performance.

Join Stock Market Forums

Participate in online forums or communities where people discuss stock market topics. You can ask questions, share your thoughts, and learn from others.

Start Small

If you decide to start investing, begin with a small amount of money that you're comfortable with. Remember that investing involves risk.

Be Patient

Learning about the stock market is a journey. Don't rush into making investments without a good understanding of what you're doing.

Remember, the stock market can be complex, so take your time to grasp the concepts. Learning gradually and building your knowledge over time will help you make informed decisions if you choose to invest in the future.

TEACHING STOCK TRADING TO KIDS

Teaching stock trading to kids requires a simplified approach that's easy for them to understand. Here are some online resources that are geared towards teaching kids about the basics of investing and stock trading:

Khan Academy - Finance and Capital Markets

Khan Academy offers a free course on finance and capital markets that covers topics like stocks, bonds, and investing. The content is presented clearly and educationally suitable for kids.

Virtual Stock Market Games

Engage kids in virtual stock market games designed to teach them about trading without using real money. These games make learning about stocks fun and interactive. Some popular options include:

- **Stock Market Game:** A program offered by the SIFMA Foundation that provides virtual trading experiences for students.
- **Investopedia Stock Simulator:** This simulator allows kids to practice trading stocks with virtual money while learning about the stock market.

BOOKS AND APPS TO HELP YOU LEARN

BOOKS

- **How to Turn $100 into $1,000,000:** Earn! Save! Invest! by James McKenna and Jeannine Glista: Provides a simple and engaging introduction to the concepts of saving, investing, and compound interest.
- **Investing For Kids:** How to Save, Invest, and Grow Money by Matthew Paladino: Explains investing concepts in a kid-friendly manner.

APPS

- **Piggybot App:** Helps kids learn about saving, spending, and giving by managing virtual money.

ONLINE EDUCATIONAL PLATFORMS

1. **Junior Achievement:** Offers various programs that teach financial literacy and entrepreneurship to kids.
2. **MyMoney.gov:** A U.S. government website providing resources for teaching kids about money and finances.
3. **YouTube Channels:**
- CrashCourse Kids - Economics and Finance: Provides educational videos on various topics, including economics and finance, suitable for young learners.
- Sesame Street - Money and Counting: Offers videos that teach young children basic concepts related to money and counting.
4. **Rich Kid Smart Kid:** Offers interactive games and lessons designed to teach kids about money, investing, and entrepreneurship.

When teaching kids about stock trading, it's important to focus on the basics, use simple language, and make it a fun learning experience. Always emphasize the importance of saving, responsible spending, and the potential risks involved in investing.

TEACHING KIDS REAL ESTATE

While real estate training for kids will need to be simplified and age-appropriate, here are some ideas to help them understand the basics:

Start with Basics
Begin by explaining what real estate is – that it's about land, buildings, and property. Use relatable examples, such as their own home or nearby buildings.

Property Types
Introduce different types of properties like homes, apartments, and commercial buildings. Explain how each type is used and what makes them unique.

Ownership and Renting
Teach them about property ownership and renting. Explain that some people own the places they live in, while others rent from owners. Use simple terms to describe the concepts of landlords, tenants, and rent.

Location, Location, Location
Introduce the importance of location in real estate. Explain how properties in different areas can have different values based on factors like schools, parks, and safety.

Buying and Selling
Simplify the process of buying and selling properties. Discuss how people can sell their property to move somewhere else, and how buying a property involves paying money to own it.

Investment
Introduce the idea of investing in real estate. Explain that some people buy properties not to live in, but to rent to others. This can help kids understand the concept of earning money from property.

Income and Expenses
Talk about how property owners earn money through rent and how they also have expenses like property taxes and maintenance costs.

Math Activities
Create simple math activities that involve budgeting, calculating expenses, and estimating potential rental income. This can make learning about real estate more interactive.

Field Trips
If possible, take kids on a visit to a real estate office or show them different types of properties in your area. This can make the concepts more tangible.

Books and Videos
Look for age-appropriate books, videos, or online resources that explain real estate concepts in a fun and engaging way.

Games
Consider playing board games or online games that simulate real estate transactions. These games can help kids understand how buying, renting, and investing in properties work.

Case Studies
Share simplified real-life case studies of how people have bought properties, rented them out, and earned income. Emphasize the decision-making process and outcomes.

Remember that the goal is to spark their interest and provide a basic understanding of real estate concepts. As they grow older, you can gradually introduce more complex ideas and encourage further exploration if they show a keen interest in real estate investing.

FUN AND EDUCATIONAL GAMES TO TEACH KIDS ABOUT REAL ESTATE

Teaching kids about real estate through games can be a fun and interactive way to introduce them to important concepts. Here are some games that you can use to teach kids about real estate:

Monopoly
This classic board game simulates real estate transactions and property management. Players buy and trade properties, collect rent, and make decisions about buying houses and hotels. It's a great way to introduce concepts like property ownership, rent, and negotiation.

Cashflow for Kids
Created by Robert Kiyosaki, the author of "Rich Dad Poor Dad," this game teaches financial literacy and includes real estate investing concepts. Players learn about income, expenses, assets, and liabilities as they move around the game board.

The Game of Life
This board game allows players to experience different life paths, including careers, family, and housing decisions. It's a way to introduce the idea of choosing between buying a house and renting, and making financial decisions.

Real Estate Tycoon
This game allows players to buy, sell, and manage properties, making strategic decisions to earn money and grow their real estate empire. It's available in various formats, including board games and digital versions.

SimCity
While not exclusively about real estate, this city-building simulation game lets players create and manage their own cities. They must make decisions about zoning, infrastructure, and property development, giving them a taste of urban planning and property management.

Landlord
This mobile app game uses real-world locations and properties. Players buy virtual properties, upgrade them, and compete against others in their area. It's a modern twist on the classic Monopoly concept.

Build a Lot
In this video game series, players buy, develop, and sell properties. They also manage rental properties and make decisions about improvements. It's a hands-on way to learn about property development and management.

Capital City
This board game involves players competing to build the most valuable city by acquiring properties and making strategic decisions about development and investment.

Property Mogul
A simple online game that lets players buy and sell properties, make improvements, and manage their virtual real estate portfolio.

House Flipper
While not specifically for kids, this video game lets players renovate and "flip" virtual properties for profit. It can teach about home improvement, design, and making investment decisions.

Remember to choose games that are appropriate for the age and understanding level of the kids you're teaching. Games that involve decision-making, negotiation, and resource management can help them grasp the concepts of real estate investing and property management in an enjoyable way.

ADDITIONAL RESOURCES

There are several resources available for parents who are supporting kid entrepreneurs. These resources can provide guidance, tips, and tools to help you navigate the unique challenges and opportunities that come with nurturing a young businessperson. Here are some valuable resources to consider:

1. **Target Evolution Inc.:** Target Evolution is an after-school and summer youth entrepreneurship program that provides teens with training and opportunities to sell products in major retail stores and shopping malls nationwide. They provide an online curriculum, workbooks, a Teen Biz Box with product inventory for kids to sell, and pop-up shops and vendor opportunities.
2. **NFTE (Network for Teaching Entrepreneurship):** NFTE offers programs that teach entrepreneurship skills to young people from under-resourced communities. They provide curricula, competitions, and mentorship opportunities to help students start and run their own businesses.
3. **Junior Achievement (JA):** Junior Achievement provides programs that focus on financial literacy, entrepreneurship, and work readiness for students at various age levels. Their resources can help parents and educators support young entrepreneurs' learning journey.
4. **Young Entrepreneurs Academy (YEA!):** YEA! offers entrepreneurship education programs for students in middle and high school. They provide curricula, mentorship, and resources to help young entrepreneurs develop and launch their own businesses.
5. **Books:** There are numerous books written specifically for young entrepreneurs and their parents. Some recommendations include "Kid Start-Up" by Mark Cuban, "Better Than a Lemonade Stand" by Daryl Bernstein, and "How to Be an Entrepreneur" by DK.
6. **Online Courses:** Platforms like Udemy, Coursera, and LinkedIn Learning offer online courses on entrepreneurship and business basics. Some courses are tailored for young entrepreneurs and their parents.
7. **Local Business Organizations:** Check if your local chamber of commerce or small business development center offers resources or workshops for young entrepreneurs. They might provide networking events, educational sessions, and mentorship opportunities.
8. **YouTube Channels:** Many YouTube channels focus on entrepreneurship and business education. Some channels specifically target young entrepreneurs and provide practical advice, success stories, and tips.
9. **Entrepreneurship Camps:** Look for local or online entrepreneurship camps designed for kids and teenagers. These camps often provide hands-on experiences, workshops, and networking opportunities.
10. **Podcasts:** There are podcasts that discuss entrepreneurship from various perspectives, including those geared toward young entrepreneurs. "Kidpreneurs Podcast" is an example of a podcast that interviews and features young entrepreneurs.
11. **Startup Competitions:** Keep an eye out for startup competitions and challenges that welcome young entrepreneurs. These events provide a platform for kids to showcase their ideas and gain exposure.
12. **Online Communities:** Online forums and communities, such as social media groups or dedicated websites, can connect parents of kid entrepreneurs. You can share experiences, ask questions, and learn from each other.
13. **Local Mentors and Business Owners:** Reach out to local entrepreneurs, business owners, and professionals who might be willing to mentor your child. Personal connections can provide valuable insights and guidance.

Teen Biz Parent Guide

www.ingramcontent.com/pod-product-compliance
Lightning Source LLC
Chambersburg PA
CBRC091726070526
44586CB00008B/83